"This is a wonderful account of the poverty wars of the 1960s as they unfolded in Mingo County, West Virginia. Inspired (and funded) by the federal war on poverty, the presumably apathetic Appalachian poor mobilized with gusto. And so did the challenged local power structure. Read this book to learn about this moment of American history."

—Frances Fox Piven,
Professor Political Science and Sociology, City University of New York
and author of *Poor People's Movements : Why They Succeed, How They Fail*

"Huey Perry's account of the War on Poverty in West Virginia is a classic. Nothing I have read gives such an insider's account of both of the promise of LBJ's initiative, and the way this hope was largely subverted by state and local politicians and coal companies. The book is, as well, a quirky, funny page-turner. I was hugely indebted to this book while writing my novel *The Unquiet Earth*. WVU Press is to be commended for keeping this important account available both to historians and the general public."

—Denise Giardina,
author of *Storming Heaven* and *The Unquiet Earth*

Praise for the first edition

"Perry's story, told simply and without polemics, shows how hard it is to do something that seems simple—get funds into the hands of the poor."

—Edward Magnuson, *Time* magazine

"This book is one of those unexpected delights that comes along every once in a while, but not often enough."

—*New Republic*

"They'll Cut Off Your Project"

WEST VIRGINIA AND APPALACHIA

A series edited By Ronald L. Lewis, Ken Fones-Wolf, and Kevin Barksdale

VOLUME 13

Other books in the series:

An Appalachian Reawakening:
West Virginia and the Perils of the New Machine Age, 1945-1972
By Jerry Bruce Thomas

An Appalachian New Deal: West Virginia in the Great Depression
By Jerry Bruce Thomas

Culture, Class, and Politics in Modern Appalachia
Edited by Jennifer Egolf, Ken Fones-Wolf,
and Louis C. Martin

Governor William E. Glasscock and Progressive Politics in West Virginia
By Gary Jackson Tucker

Matewan Before the Massacre
By Rebecca J. Bailey

Sectionalism in Virginia from 1776 to 1881, Second Edition
By Charles Ambler
Introduction to the second edition by Barbara Rasmussen

Monongah: The Tragic Story
of the 1907 Monongah Mine Disaster
By Davitt McAteer

continued in back of book

"THEY'LL CUT OFF YOUR PROJECT"

A MINGO COUNTY CHRONICLE

HUEY PERRY

West Virginia University Press
Morgantown 2011

West Virginia University Press, Morgantown 26506
2011 West Virginia University Press

Second edition published 2011 by West Virginia University Press
First edition published 1972 Praeger Publishers, Inc.

19 18 17 16 15 14 13 12 11   9 8 7 6 5 4 3 2 1

cloth: 1-933202-80-7
978-1-933202-80-8
paper: 1-933202-79-3
978-1-933202-79-2

Library of Congress Catalog Card Number: 72-75692

Printed in the United States of America

To the grandchildren,

Hallie Cross, Josie Cross, Janie Cross, Madison Perry, and Stewart Perry.

"May you always remember your roots."

Foreword

Huey Perry's War

Standing on the streets of Williamson, West Virginia in the winter of 1966, Huey Perry dazzled a *New York Times* reporter with the achievements of his native Mingo County's thirty community action programs. Roads into the back hollows had been repaired; schoolhouses had been renovated. Carpenters assisted by men on relief had torn down abandoned shacks and built and painted new homes. Swimming pools had been fixed; a park overlooking the dramatic valleys had been built.

As director of the county's antipoverty program, Perry swelled with his pride in his work.

"This must be the most beautiful community action group in the nation," Perry told the *Times*.

Thanks to Perry's tour, the reporter noted that six-hundred children now attended Head Start classes, three-hundred teenagers took part in self-help employment projects, and medical checkups had become routine.

The crowning achievement, which had garnered the headlines for the story, rested with the new grocery store: "Poor in West Virginia Town, Worried About the High Price of Food, Open Own Grocery."

Perry called it, "poor power." By taking over an abandoned store and selling shares at ten dollars a shot, unemployed residents in the area had refashioned the shelves into a community grocery store, which ultimately had triggered a sharp reduction in food prices.

For the thirty-year-old Perry, described as "a tall, rangy young man," by the *Times* reporter, it was "important for the poor to mobilize their resources collectively."

The story takes a turn here: The reporter did not buy completely into the storybook idealism unfolding on the back streets of Williamson and in the tiny settlements of Big Branch and Cinderella. She had been sent to Mingo County to chronicle the controversy as much as the accomplishments.

"Grocers are angry," the reporter noted. "Other businessmen are uneasy. Old line politicians are upset." The local state senator and members of the Chamber of Commerce had already gone to Washington, charging that the Mingo County antipoverty program "was attempting to create a political machine by mobilizing the poor."

Federal investigators had already arrived. A local businessman told the *Times*: "It's all a Communist plot."

Although Huey Perry had only been director for a year, his immediate troubles appeared to be under control. But as the *Times* reporter foretold, the "political trouble still smolders quietly in the Harvey district, where the poor have revolted against the politically powerful local Democratic family who controlled the area."

In effect, Huey Perry's real troubles had just begun.

Books on the War on Poverty abound, and books on the Appalachian region certainly seem to have cornered the market on the poverty program's most dramatic if not agonizingly tragic moments in our contemporary studies. Nonetheless, while other regions entrenched in economic depressions existed elsewhere in the country, Appalachia emerged as the "ideal proving grounds," according to historian Ron Eller, for President Lyndon B. Johnson's "crusade to eliminate poverty" in the 1960s.

Hence, the War on Poverty is the story of Appalachia's twisted years of economic despair and political machinations and genuine acts of rebellion and reform.

In his classic history of modern Appalachia, *Uneven Ground: Appalachia Since 1945*, Eller depicts the great poverty campaign launched in 1964 as a paradox of "idealism and compromise," blending the "popular ideas" of the era into "vagaries of the national politics and intellectual trends of the day." As ground zero in our nation's rediscovery of poverty in America, Appalachia became central to Johnson's vision for a more equitable economic playing field. As the antipoverty program unfolded, Eller adds: "Appalachia increasingly became the yardstick against which to measure government success in the War on Poverty. Not only was Appalachia on the front lines for the EOA [Economic Opportunity Act] but it was also the only American region to receive a special program for infrastructure development."

They'll Cut Off Your Project, Huey Perry's extraordinary memoir, takes place on those Appalachian frontlines of the War on Poverty. More importantly, it stands out today as one of the most enduring chronicles on this still unfinished chapter in Appalachian and American social history.

Published by Praeger in New York City in 1972, on the heels of Perry's five-year tenure as director of an upstart Economic Opportunity Commission project in Mingo County, West Virginia, the memoir provides a rare window into the foibles and triumphs of Perry's groundbreaking role as an antipoverty pioneer.

In fact, lamenting that stacks of treatises and more politically motivated portraits of the War on Poverty and Appalachia's raggedy role needlessly packed the bookstore shelves and college reading lists, the *Saturday Review* highlighted Perry's memoir as a singular achievement in its day. The *Review* found Perry's account to be "as vivid and personal a book as one could ask for." The magazine praised the memoir for its "plain, straightforward report."

Time Magazine echoed such praise. In a time of inflamed tensions and lingering controversy over the poverty programs and political upheaval, *Time* found Perry's ability to write "simply and without polemics" to be a refreshing narrative on how the antipoverty campaign tried to do "something that seems simple—get the funds into the hands of the poor."

In essence: How did the War on Poverty go wrong? That festering question still resonates today, making the clarity of Perry's enduring book an even more important portal into the backstories of the confusing era, if not a timeless cautionary tale of good intentions in a land of greed and political corruption.

Failing to succumb to the political rhetoric of the times, *They'll Cut Off Your Project* functions as much as an antimemoir as it does as a memoir, or as French author Andre Malraux once posited, it answers "questions that other memoirs do not ask, and does not answer those they do." For Perry, like Malraux, "what was at stake went deeper than politics."

"The war on poverty had been declared in Appalachia," Perry writes in his first chapter. "Before long, Mingo County was to become one of its battlefields, with me, a high school history teacher up to the time this chronicle begins, smack dab in the middle of it."

How on earth Perry ended up right smack dab in the middle of these political hijinks must have been on his mind one early morning in 1970. Five years into his job as director, recognized by politicians and local citizens alike as the "leader of the poor," of whom many concluded "there would be no more problems in the county" if he could somehow be "eliminated," Perry found himself surrounded by a half-dozen armed federal marshals and FBI agents. Investigating the misuse of federal funds and possible election tampering, the agents handed Perry a subpoena for his EOC office records.

Knowing that he was being investigated on trumped up charges concocted by politicians and local business leaders who were threatened by the success and empowerment activities of the community action projects, Perry quipped to the agents that their disgraceful treatment was what he had come to "expect when you help the poor."

Perry had learned a lot about helping the poor in the five years prior to this investigation, and those lessons largely came by trial and error. Taking the job with virtually no training in 1965, Perry recalls in his memoir how even a Mingo County native like himself was not fully prepared for the extent of poverty, and its entanglement in local politics, in the back hollers and abandoned coal camps of Appalachia.

"Although I had lived in Appalachia all of my life," Perry writes, "I was stunned by the conditions that I saw during the initial weeks of looking into hollows of Mingo. The visible effects of poverty were everywhere—the shacks, the filth, the pale, pot-bellied babies, the miners with silicosis, coughing and gasping for breath, the outhouses, the dirt roads, and the one-room schools. Up and down the hollows, the front yards were strewn with junked cars, and the seats from abandoned automobiles were used for beds and sofas."

Even as one of the top coal-producing areas in central Appalachia, 50 percent of the population in Mingo County lived in poverty; one out of five was a welfare recipient. Half of the homes were substandard, and many were without plumbing. Infant mortality ranked higher than anywhere else in the country.

With the boom and bust mode of coal mining in full effect, Mingo County suffered greatly from increasing mechanization, which discounted the need for more miners. Automation blues. Most miners remained in the area until their unemployment benefits were exhausted, and then they took to the road for jobs in the factories in the Midwest or beyond. Mingo County had lost 16 percent of its population in the decade prior to when Perry came aboard.

Without a doubt, Perry faced a desperate situation of powerlessness among his charged constituents.

Taking the Economic Opportunity Act of 1964 on its stated promise, Perry immediately invoked the Act's main phrase:

"To involve the poor to the maximum extent possible."

His strategy: Organize community action groups. And what were "community action groups" asked Perry's colleagues?

"A community action group would consist of low-income citizens organized together to identify their problems and work toward possible solutions." Most importantly, Perry adds: "I feel it is necessary that we take our time and build an organization that involves the poor in the decisions as to what types of programs they want, rather than to sit down and write up what we think they want."

From the first day on the job, Perry made it clear that he was not in the business of social work, but personal and community empowerment through action.

In one of their first meetings, Perry set the ambitious goal that would inspire poverty programs around the nation and scare the daylights out of the old power structure in his homeland: "If we can change the conditions of Mingo County, perhaps the whole state of West Virginia can be changed. We should work to make this a model for the rest of Appalachia to follow."

Perry was not artless. He recognized a systematic stacking of the deck against community residents who lived in a county where the majority of the mineral rights were in the hands of outside corporations.

The challenge for Perry, therefore, was that the "people were powerless to counteract the avalanche of individual and community problems inflicted upon them by the selfish economic system that had been organized to remove coal and timber, leaving the area devoid of wealth."

And there was another problem: Noah Floyd, the local political boss, whose family had ruled the area for generations, and his henchman T.I. Varney, who pulled the edge of his coat back on their first meeting and showed off his .38 revolver.

As historian Dwight Billings notes in *The Road to Poverty: The Making of Hardship in Appalachia*, Perry's experience was hardly unique in central Appalachia. Douglas Arnett chronicled a similar struggle "to control 'community action' in Clay County, Kentucky" in that same period via another countywide government agency. Echoing Perry's analysis of the local power brokers, Arnett concluded that "the local elite was willing to tolerate the work of the development association as long as the innovations were merely 'functioning innovations' and not 're-structuring innovations' which would threaten the social structure."

Not that Perry intentionally set out on a threatening path.

His introduction into this rigid social structure was as unassuming and sincere as his prose. Even the *New York Times* reporter in 1966 concluded the same about Perry's persona. He was not an "outsider" who had come in to "stir up the poor." Perry demanded that the VISTA workers—arriving as domestic Peace Corps volunteers from outside the region— cut their long hair and dress to local standards.

Raised in the small settlement of Gilbert Creek in Mingo County, Perry first learned of President Johnson's celebrated visit to the central Appalachian coalfields and his plans for the War on Poverty on his parent's front porch, in the house where he had been born and raised. On a summer break from his seventh year of teaching high school, as hundreds of antipoverty jobs sprang up in the region, Perry almost casually opted to apply for the position of executive director of his county's new Economic Opportunity Commission. The job appeared like a nice departure from his summer work on a used car lot. The issue of poverty concerned him. And to his surprise, Perry was selected to become the new director.

Making a comparison with northern missionaries who flooded into Appalachia after the Civil War and during Reconstruction, historian John Alexander Williams places Perry's eventual encounters with controversy as "inherent in any program that involved better service to poor people whose prior access to government programs had been through gatekeepers tied into local power structures."

Appalachian in the 1960s was no different. A new generation rediscovered Appalachia and sent its missionaries, now in the guise of government poverty warriors, to entangle themselves in the complexities of impoverishment—that is, displaced and deracinated residents hemmed in by limited possibilities in an extraction economy and by welfare dependency.

Because of his very nature to look elsewhere for change, Perry began a clean break with the local chieftains. Perry writes with ease about the daily efforts to lift community people to their feet to simply embark on the rebellious act of holding public meetings.

In his historical overview of West Virginia, Williams praises Perry's chronicle as a "detailed and entertaining" example of "how the poverty program unsettled established authorities."

Even Perry's Mingo roots, marking him as a local instead

of an intruding "outsider" or a patronizing poverty warrior, as Williams points out in his classic text, *Appalachia: A History*, did not prevent the Mingo County native son from clashing with the "county's notoriously corrupt political structure headed by state senator Noah Floyd, representing the last generation of his powerful and historic family."

For Floyd, Perry's role in organizing a public hearing for Harvey District Community Action Group was treasonous enough. In the memoir, Floyd pulls Perry aside and reads him the riot act: "Now, I don't know, Perry, what has inspired you to call such a meeting, but you're gonna tear up everything here in this county with this kind of thing."

This kind of thing, of course, referred to community involvement in the new poverty funds, as opposed to the dictates of Floyd and a handful of businessmen and local politicians. Once Floyd's dreaded public hearing began, people took to the rostrum and questioned—for the first time—how public monies had been misused.

"Now, I'm not an educated man," begins one participant, discussing a jobs program, "and we're wanting to know why these men can't be used to work on community projects that'll benefit the community rather than just a few individuals here and there."

Imbued with the passion incited by the War on Poverty, as much as its stated purpose, the native son Perry ultimately realized that any progress for empowerment had to come at the expense of the powerful. In the process, Perry began to draw on the historical experiences that Williams notes to directly confront the systematic barriers keeping people impoverished. Within a short time, Perry saw the need to go beyond the conditions and to look at the root causes of poverty.

He writes: "The strategy was to direct the energies of the poor, away from the development and implementation of federal programs, which usually treated only the symptoms of poverty, toward the building of a political base from which the poor could attack poverty itself."

And herein lay the crisis for the old guard: Perry was slowly building a participatory democracy that would overthrow decades of corruption.

It is important to note, as Eller states in *Uneven Ground*, that Perry's conflicts grew incrementally with his successes. The *New York Times* story revealed that success to the world. The TV cameras added more tension.

And for readers, *They'll Cut Off Your Project* serves as a remarkable and triumphant testimony of strategy and tactics and overall community organizing, as much as it demonstrates the perils of challenging a corrupt system in a place with little democracy. Eller states: "At least at the onset of the War on Poverty, mountain power brokers welcomed the new federal programs and assumed that funding would be administered through state and local governments in the pattern established by the New Deal."

But when advocates like Perry eventually "organized a political action league and a fair elections committee and established an independent grocery that threatened local political and business interests."

Well, then, the real war began.

Without struggle, there is no progress, as Frederick Douglass was apt to say, and so Perry's five-year roller coaster at the helm of the antipoverty programs in Mingo County saw plenty of struggle in the midst of progress. And even violent strife.

In *They'll Cut off Your Project*, when one of Perry's colleagues is nearly trapped after a defiant meeting in a dark tunnel, infamous for mysterious murders, the Mingo County native recalls his father's stories about the "threats and violence that accompanied the movement to unionize the miners in the 1900s."

This connection between the coal wars and Perry's own poverty wars grounds the book in an important historical context. For virtually all residents in the area, the union battles would have been the closest experience to any kind of community organizing in their lifetimes.

Mingo County, in fact, shared an important strand of history with neighboring Logan County, the site of the famous Battle at Blair Mountain in 1921, when thousands of union coal miners (many of them World War I veterans) marched to "liberate" the two southwestern counties of West Virginia in an attempt to break the stranglehold of outside nonunion coal companies. With pitched battles, covered by war correspondents from the nation's largest newspapers, the Battle of Blair Mountain ended up being the largest armed insurrection since the Civil War; private airplanes were even employed to drop bombs. In the end, the miners retreated after the US military was called in to halt the fighting. It would be another decade before unions were officially recognized in the area, though the national memory of the miners' defiance on Blair Mountain remained a badge of pride for the area's residents.

Yet, while threats continued over various projects, Walter Cronkite's TV news crew made multiple visits, and the community action groups continued to grow with self-confidence and progressed in employment, school participation, and housing repair, among many projects. So entrenched politicians turned to their bigger weapon: Governor Hulett Smith.

If the local chieftains could not control Perry or his funds or community action groups, then they would simply shift jurisdiction to their county courts.

As Perry narrates, while he and his Mingo County parents are dealing with the issue of hot lunches at the local schools, Gov. Smith has quietly introduced legislation granting the county courts control over the authority of the poverty programs. In an emergency session, the bill overwhelmingly passed in favor of the local courts, which were controlled by the local politicians.

As the legal counsel for the Fair Election's Committee later noted: "There was no emergency whatsoever for this bill. It was a move for politicians in southern counties to take over poverty programs so they could put the poor people in line. The Mingo EOC has been regarded as a national model by the OEO [Office of Economic Opportunities] for the poor's war on poverty. What worries me is that the efforts of poor people in Mingo County to correct problems will be killed by the same people who caused them."

Perry and his action groups leapt into action. Realizing that politicians understood power, they sought the endorsement of their poverty programs by the opposing Republican Party candidate for governor in the upcoming election. At the same time, Perry's troops began the process of organizing a mass rally—including a hearse, to signify the death of the poverty program if it shifted into the hands of the county courts—while waiting for the gubernatorial candidates to respond. Just as the convoy was readying to depart for the Charleston capital, the governor relinquished his earlier move and agreed to follow the power of designation under federal law.

Perry's program was saved. But the controversies, including the FBI raid, would continue.

By the end of Perry's five-year term at the EOC, the four main opposing politicians would be brought to trial for election fraud and buying votes. None of the accused would be found guilty. Perry, meanwhile, had taken a new job in a low-income housing program in Charleston.

Befitting his style and experience, Perry attempts to end the book on a cautionary tone, quoting one of his political nemeses at the trial: "I thank God we still have justice in this country."

After going through five years of social justice battles on the frontlines of the War on Poverty, Perry certainly intends for his reader to question the very meaning of the terms of justice in our nation.

Tucked into the southwest corner of West Virginia, Mingo County still struggles today with many of the same issues of community displacement and disempowerment, poverty, unemployment, and poor health care. Nearly 30 percent of the population live with income under the poverty level, compared to 18 percent for the rest of the state; unemployment hovers at 10 percent.

Coal mining, though even more mechanized than in Perry's era in the 1970s, provides one out of five jobs in the county. In 2008, Mingo County counted 1,700 jobs related to the coal industry out of 8,600 employed workers in the area. That same year, a Gallup health care survey on the "well-being rankings" among congressional districts found the community in Mingo County ranked 434 out of 435 districts.

Statistics, of course, hardly tell the full story.

As the *Human Behavior* journal noted in its review of *They'll Cut Off Your Project*, Perry's memoir told his own personal story and also transcended his own personal story to introduce readers to another side of Appalachia—an Appalachia that had already been stereotyped for over a century for its enduring poverty and beholden to an inexorable cultural-of-poverty inertia manifested into the moonshine-swilling lazy hillbilly tucked back into the hollers of yesteryear.

Just as Perry was taking the reins of his position in 1965–1966, an influential study on Appalachian poverty and society, detailing the region's "pathological" disinterest in community action, was pressed into the hands of every poverty worker, journalist, and politician. *Yesterday's People: Life in Contemporary Appalachia* by Jack Weller casts mountaineers as "stubborn, sullen, and perverse" people in a region where there was "no rebellion, little questioning, little complaining." Nearly bereft of any analysis of the political and corporate corruption and control in the extraction-economy-based communities, Weller instead points at the folk culture of the Appalachians, such as those in Mingo County, as the stumbling block, impeding the mountaineers' ability to "foster the human values of personal worth, dignity, responsibility, and happiness." For Weller, and many poverty warriors of the period, the Appalachians simply possessed an "instability of character" that would not allow for community action.

On the other hand, the Appalachia's folk culture, for Appalachian labor activist, educator, and author Don West, had served as the bulwark of resistance and community action in Appalachia for over a century. He charges in his pamphlet in 1969, "Romantic Appalachia: Poverty Pays If You Ain't Poor," that missionaries like Weller followed a cyclical tradition of "discovering" Appalachian poverty and mores. West writes: "Yes, the southern mountains have been missionarized, researched and studied, surveyed, romanticized, dramatized, hillbillyized, Dogpatchized, and povertyized again." For West, the War on Poverty overlooked the actual causes of poverty and "never intended to end poverty. That would require a total reconstruction of the system of ownership, production and the distribution of wealth."

In many respects, West's admonition informed the uniqueness of Perry's work and writing. West warned: "The 'missionaries'—religious or secular—had and have one thing in common: they didn't trust us hill folk to speak, plan, and act for ourselves. Bright, articulate, ambitious, well-intentioned, they become our spokesmen, our planners, our actors. And so they'll go again, leaving us and our poverty behind. But is there a lesson to be learned from all these outside efforts that have failed to save us? I think so."

For West, native mountaineers like Perry needed to "organize and save ourselves. . . . We must learn to organize again, speak, plan, and act for ourselves."

For the social science journal *Human Behavior*, Perry's memoir uniquely served that role, both in providing the insights of a native Appalachia into the complexities of poverty and community action, and in giving voice to disenfranchised Appalachians typically left out of the discussion on development. In its review of *They'll Cut Off Your Project*, the journal praised Perry for seeing "both sides" of the poverty dilemma. "As one of nine children born to a former coal miner in Mingo County, West Virginia, where his parents still live on Gilbert Creek, Perry writes with pride and understanding of his people."

Allowing for personal stories and portraits to emerge in his narrative, Perry's memoir defies Weller's dismissal of rural community action without having to resort to any political rhetoric or manifesto; at the same time, Perry underscores West's concern about the corporate control of the region by examining the impact of a county's economy beholden to the single boom-bust coal industry, but goes one step further than West by being willing to challenge the corruptive influence of native politicians and rural power brokers who had openly manipulated and exploited residents for decades. For Perry, the great obstacle to the elimination of poverty was not simply a matter of outside corporate dominance or meddling missionaries, but the local political machine in Mingo County, "which manipulated elections to maintain control."

In this respect, *They'll Cut Off Your Project* is almost less Perry's personal story than the collective narrative of the Mingo County residents—from both sides—who made the War on Poverty their own private battlefield for community action.

And the nation watched the fallout, often drawing their own narrow conclusions.

As readers, we are lucky enough to transcend the media stereotypes and be invited into the world of mothers and fathers, the unemployed and those on relief, and the dogged and fledging community action groups that overcame generations of abuse to rise up against the power structure and demand a say in their community. They have names, lives, children, hopes, and foibles. As Perry quietly narrates the story, the very town and hollow players who enthralled the *New York Times* reporter in 1966 ultimately become the protagonists in Mingo County's extraordinary experiment with participatory democracy.

This story not only resonated with the nation in 1972, when readers first peered into Perry's Appalachian coal camps, small towns, and hollows, but also remains an important factor in any movement for social justice and sustainable economies today—especially in Mingo County.

At the same time that Perry chronicles the collapse of labor-intensive coal mining and forewarns both the demise of the United Mine Worker union and the flight of labor and once stable communities, he also places his own project within the context of a region lacking any diversification of the economy. Well into the twenty-first century, that phenomenon for the coalfield region of central Appalachia remains the main enduring crisis for its residents.

Such a phenomenon begs the question: Should economic diversification be the focus of community action groups in their struggle to eradicate the current entrenched poverty in Mingo County and Appalachia?

For Eric Mathis, an economist and director of Mingo County's 2010 JOBS Project in Williamson, which seeks to develop alternative energy jobs and initiatives in the region, "Perry's classic exemplifies the conditions which we have come to know as entrenched interests and from his story we are led to believe, much like John Gaventa's conclusions in *Power and Powerlessness*, that genuinely combating poverty in Appalachia is tedious and perhaps even impossible."

Like Perry, Mathis's nationally acclaimed community project in the same areas of Mingo County seeks to "account for several factors which typically do not fall under the traditional approaches to organizing or community empowerment. In this model, power is not a continuum but a dynamic work of art where expression of meaning is based on the way we interpret the piece in question. In Mingo County, and elsewhere in the coalfields of Central Appalachia, this piece in question is simply economics and the dynamic forces which sustain these elusive systems that structure our day-to-day lives. Our approach is an economic one which calls into question the basic assumptions of the system as a whole by interlocking employees' and community stakeholders' creative capacity with those of the local elite thus interlocking the very survival of the modern-day coal town, with the interests of the people."

When Perry chronicles his work to establish a moccasin factory that would train and employ thirty-five welfare recipients, along with a gourmet restaurant and a nonprofit grocery store, thereby challenging the local business community, you can almost feel a contemporary air of unease at the clean energy and sustainable jobs projects that are emerging in our era in the central Appalachian region with local, state, and federal assistance.

Makes you wonder: Would they cut your project today, if your community action group challenged the local business and political chieftains in Mingo County with the fearlessness of Perry's colleagues in the 1960s and 1970s, or will Perry's legacy finally be vindicated?

—Jeff Biggers
September 23, 2010

1

Mrs. Musick was busy hanging out her morning wash. She took a clothespin out of her mouth and yelled across the creek to my mother, "Did you read in the paper last night where President Johnson is coming to Inez, Kentucky?"

My mother answered, "Yes, I read the article. Said he was coming all the way down here just to visit with a poor family that has ten or twelve children."

Mrs. Musick finished hanging up her last batch of clothes. They waved briskly in the wind. She yelled again to my mother, "Are you and Uley going over there to see him?"

"No, I guess not. What about you and Joe?"

"I reckon not. Me and Joe would have to hire someone to take us, and on what little welfare we get we just can't afford it."

She moved over toward the little walkway that spanned Gilbert Creek and leaned against the side railing. "To tell you the truth, I don't see why he has to come all the way here. I'm sure President Kennedy must have told him about the conditions here before he was killed."

My mother was sitting on the front step stringing beans for the evening supper. She said, "Well, I guess it's just their way of doing things."

As I recall this scene, I had been half reading a newspaper on the porch of my father's house in Mingo County, West Virginia, the same house in which I had been born nearly thirty years before, and half listening to the conversation between my mother and the neighbor. Now I laid aside the paper and entered the conversation.

"What he is attempting to do is call attention to the poverty that exists here in an effort to get the American people to do something about it."

"Well, if it will help us poor people a little, I'm all for it," Mrs. Musick said. "It sure is hard times around here since all the mines closed."

The next day, President Lyndon B. Johnson landed at the Tri-State Airport in Huntington, West Virginia, and was whisked away by helicopter to Inez, ten miles across the state line from Mingo County, where he met and talked with a genuine low income family. The network television cameras, along with a number of newspaper correspondents, were all there to relay the story to the American people. The war on poverty in Appalachia had been declared. Before long, Mingo County was to become one of its battlefields, with me, a high school history teacher up to the time this chronicle begins, smack dab in the middle of it.

When, late in 1964, the Congress of the United States passed the Economic Opportunity Act, designed to "eliminate the paradox of poverty in the midst of plenty," local governments were invited to sponsor nonprofit corporations that would submit applications for grants to the Office of Economic Opportunity, soon commonly known as the OEO. Hundreds of community action agencies sprang up overnight all over the country. Mingo's neighboring county, McDowell, had submitted an application for a million dollar federal grant even before the President had signed the bill and appointed Sargent Shriver to head the agency. Getting scent of the McDowell plum, the Mingo County Court, the county's three-man governing body, quickly established a six-man commission, made up of membership from the local Chamber of Commerce, to obtain a state charter and to apply to the OEO for a federal grant. I had been following with much interest the newspaper publicity given to the new poverty program, and, when Mingo County's newly created Economic Opportunity Commission (EOC) advertised for an executive director, I applied for the job.

It was in early June, 1965. My seventh school term had just ended, and I had started my summer job with a local car dealer. Selling used cars was not the most satisfying job, but the $300 a month came in handy—especially since the pay for a teacher with a master's degree was only $5,000 per year. At almost five o'clock on June 14, when I returned from delivering a new car the owner had sold the day before, the office girl informed me that she had received a call from Richard Cutlip, chairman of the interviewing committee of the Economic Opportunity Commission, and that I had been selected as director. This was when I became a part of the Great Society's war on poverty. It was difficult to believe. I had no political ties with the Democratic machine that controlled Mingo County, and I had not really expected to be hired when I submitted the application. I returned the call and was instructed to report to work the next day.

My first day on the job was spent mostly with Gerald

Chafin, a mortician from Delbarton, who had been appointed by the County Court to head the newly created Commission. Chafin was honest in saying that he did not know much about the job, or the program either, but to him it sounded like an opportunity to bring some money into the county. After much discussion during the morning, Chafin told me that he felt it would be wise for me to meet some of the businessmen in Williamson, because they, as members of the Chamber of Commerce, had persuaded the County Court to establish the Commission. I spent the remainder of the day meeting the county's affluent. Chafin had been quick to point out that he was my boss. He also said that he wanted me and an aide hired prior to my selection to attend a training session at Virginia Polytechnic Institute in Blacksburg, Virginia.

The aide, Jimmy Wolford, a hefty two-hundred-pounder, was well known in the Williamson area, where he had worked as a radio announcer for the local station. I met him and the secretary, Donna Hall, who had just graduated from high school, the following day at the temporary office, which had been established on the second floor of the courthouse annex.

Jimmy congratulated me warmly on my selection and said, "You know, Perry, we've got one hell of a job ahead of us, and I don't know a damn thing about it."

"I suppose we'll just have to learn as we go," I replied. "This whole business is new, and I don't suppose anyone knows much about it. Maybe we can pick up some ideas at the training session."

Changing the subject, Jimmy said, "You know, Perry, I worked with Hubert Humphrey in his campaign here in West Virginia in 1960 when he run against John F. Kennedy. I don't know whether you have heard of me or not,

4

but I got some records out. Course, in the campaign, I would play and sing and loosen the crowd up before Hubert would make his speech. I'll tell you, he is a smart man, and I know he had a lot to do in getting the poverty act passed before Congress." Without hesitating, he added, "There is a book out called *The Making of a President, 1960*, and there are two pages devoted to me about playing music for Humphrey, and, of course, it describes me when Hubert made his concession speech to Kennedy in Charleston. You know, it was a damn shame he lost."

"Sounds like you have had some interesting experiences."

"Oh, I sure have, and I can tell you a lot about these politicians here in Mingo, and, believe me, we are going to have to watch our step. We don't want to do anything that will upset them. You know, if we can keep Noah Floyd happy, we will be in good shape."

We chatted a few minutes longer, finally making plans to leave the following morning for the training session. There we spent the next two weeks listening to a sociologist talking about group dynamics and to OEO employees explaining guidelines and the procedures to follow in writing a proposal. However, very little direction was given, and I concluded that, if there was to be a direction, we would have to develop it ourselves. Jimmy continued to tell me and the other trainees about Hubert Humphrey and, at one point, acquired a guitar and sang several campaign songs that he had written. I felt that I had learned more about Hubert Humphrey during those two weeks than about how to operate and develop a poverty program.

On the day we returned from the training session, Chafin called a special meeting of the Board of Directors of the EOC so that we might give a report. The eighteen-member board consisted of the County Court's six representatives, one representative from each of the county's four towns and the city of Williamson, and representatives from such organizations as civic groups and women's clubs. At 7:00 P.M., Chafin called the meeting to order and announced that he had received a telegram from the Office of Economic Opportunity stating that an $18,160 program development grant had been awarded to the Commission. Since the evening paper had run a large headline article to that effect, it was not news, but everyone appeared to be well pleased with the announcement.

When Jimmy and I gave our brief reports on the training session, the only significant thing I could say was that we had to have "people development" before program development and that I had no plans to submit any proposals to Washington until we had a chance to talk with the poor people of the county to see what they wanted. To this, there was a somewhat negative response from one of the board members as he reminded me that our neighboring county, McDowell, had already received a million dollars and that there shouldn't be any reason why we couldn't do the same thing.

Sensing that I might have an immediate problem with the Board of Directors, I explained that we had been instructed by the OEO to organize the poor into community action groups before we attempted to write proposals.

"What do you mean by a community action group?" asked Chafin.

"A community action group would consist of low income citizens organized together to identify their problems and work toward possible solutions. I feel it is necessary that we take our time and build an organization that involves the poor in the decisions as to what types of programs they

6

want, rather than to sit down and write up what we think they want. If we do it the latter way, we will be no different from the welfare department or any other old-line agency that imposes ideas upon the people. Just give us some time, and we will get you some money. Just because McDowell County received a million dollars doesn't mean poverty will be eliminated overnight."

Chafin then had the Commission secretary, Margaret McQueen, who represented the Williamson Women's Club, read a letter from the OEO requesting that the Commission place at least four poor people on the board.

Virgil Marcum, an insurance salesman and one of the six members appointed by the County Court, was the first to respond: "I really don't see anything wrong with that if that's what they want. But I think we ought to be careful and make sure we get four good ones. Does anyone know somebody that wouldn't cause us any trouble?"

From the back of the room, a tall, slim, gray-haired man in his late sixties rose to his feet and asked for recognition. "Mr. Chairman, we have got a bus driver by the name of Donnie Browning who would make a good one, and I am sure I could handle him." The man was O. T. Kent, a member of the Board of Education.

There appeared to be an immediate consensus that it would be safe to place Browning on the board, and the remaining three were selected in the same fashion. Chafin then adjourned the meeting so that Jimmy and I could give a report to the Chamber of Commerce, which was in session two blocks up the street.

During the next few days, I gave serious thought to the approach that community action would take in Mingo. It

7

appeared that I had two alternatives: Either I could work with the existing political establishment in the county and satisfy their wishes or I could ignore them as much as possible and take the program directly to the people. If I chose the latter approach, then it was obvious that the greatest resistance would eventually come from the entrenched Democratic machine, which was completely controlled by Noah Floyd, the state senator from Mingo and McDowell counties. It was being rumored that Noah, an ambitious man, was interested in unseating Jim Kee from Congress in West Virginia's Fifth Congressional District. If so, it would certainly be an uphill battle. The Kees had been in control of the Fifth District since 1932. First there was John Kee, Jim's father, who died in the 1950's. He was succeeded by his wife, Elizabeth, who served until 1962, when she stepped aside in favor of their son, Jim. Jim was now serving his second term and had won both elections by a landslide.

The Floyd family was one of the early pioneer families in the county. Noah's uncle "Blind Billy" Adair had ruled the Board of Education for years until he was finally ousted after the local press had exposed his corrupt regime, reporting that all school personnel were having to pay kickbacks in order to hold their jobs. Noah's older brother had served as county superintendent at the time.

When Floyd came into power, he surrounded himself with many of the same people and families who had been in control for the past thirty years. He knew that, as long as he could control the executive committee of the county Democratic Party, he would be safe, and all sixteen members of the executive committee worked for either the county or the state. Therefore, any resistance to his decisions could immediately be destroyed through his patronage system. Although he did not completely control the school board, there was an alliance—especially on election day. In addition, he was highly respected by the local Chamber of Commerce. As a member of the state Senate, he could always arrange for meetings with the Governor or the Commissioner of State Roads when a delegation of businessmen wished to go to the state capitol in Charleston. Although Floyd appeared to be all powerful, many people felt that he was, in fact, only a front for the large absentee land owners, such as United States Steel, which itself owned one-third of the county. Certainly the utility companies, the Norfolk & Western Railroad (usually called the N & W) and local merchants made considerable impact on his decisions.

The man Floyd had ousted as party chairman had had to play a different political ballgame. In his time, the United Mine Workers was the powerful force. But the few mines that didn't close down in the late 1950's were automated, and most of the miners stayed in the county only until they used up their unemployment insurance. Thereafter, there was a major migration to the cities, particularly Columbus and Detroit. According to the 1960 census, Mingo's population decreased 16 per cent between 1950 and 1960 to a total of 39,600. Those men who did not leave were mostly placed on the AFDCU* program, which was administered by the state Department of Welfare and was more commonly known as the "crash program"; people on this program earned a dollar an hour cutting weeds along the state highways or digging graves for their neighbors. The union no longer counted. Floyd knew that he must cater to big

* Aid to Families with Dependent Children of the Unemployed.

9

business and local merchants in order to maintain his power and prestige.

I had talked with only a few welfare recipients when it became evident how much they feared Floyd and his machine. When Floyd's name was mentioned, they immediately became silent or changed the subject. In every district, Floyd had one of his men in charge of the AFDCU enrollees, and there had been cases reported where they were cut from the program after they spoke out against the machine. The men evidently learned early to keep quiet.

The phrase in the Economic Opportunity Act of 1964 "involving the poor to the maximum extent feasible" seemed to me to mean that the poor must be organized into groups within their communities. By such organization, each poor person would have an opportunity to determine what his needs were and to participate in decisions that would affect him and his community. This approach to the problems seemed logical and would make it easier to develop the types of programs poor people would respond to. I discussed it with Jimmy, whose initial reaction was "God damn, it sounds great! But I don't know what the Commission or Noah Floyd is going to say about it. You know they are going to be watching us like a hawk, and, if we get too close to the people, the politicians are going to get worried."

I told Jimmy that I was aware of the potential threat from the politicians, but, if the poor were ever to pull themselves out of poverty, they must develop the guts and courage to speak out against its causes. I added, "And remember, we are not here to treat the symptoms; we are here to destroy the causes, and I believe the political and economic system is one of the chief causes. As long as Floyd

10

controls the poor through the state and county governments and the local welfare department, how can we ever reach them?"

Jimmy was listening very carefully, and for a moment I felt almost as if I were back in the classroom. I continued, "If we can change the conditions in Mingo County, perhaps the whole state of West Virginia can be changed. We should work to make this a model for the rest of Appalachia to follow. You know, we are not that much different from eastern Kentucky and other areas of Appalachia."

For a time, Jimmy remained silent, sitting with his head propped between his hands, leaning over and staring at the floor. Then, slowly raising his head and turning his swivel chair around, he looked across the Tug River into Pike County, Kentucky. Only the river separated Mingo County from the state of Kentucky. "You know, Perry, I am willing to give it a try. I don't know much how you do it, but you know very well I can talk, and, if you will help me out a little as to what I should say to the people, I am ready to start."

Later in the day after we had that conversation, I told Jimmy that I would pacify Noah and the Commission and asked him not to attempt to explain our strategies to anyone who might relay them. Since I did not really know this man in whom I had confided or what his associations with the power structure were, I knew I had made a major decision in saying what I had. If I were wrong, I knew Noah would come bursting into my office the minute he learned. My biggest job was not to let him know, or at least to have a good answer that he would have to accept, if and when he found out what we were doing.

After Jimmy and the secretary left, I turned off the lights

and locked the office. As I turned the corner toward the elevator, Noah walked past, accompanied by T. I. Varney, the county's probation and parole officer. They both spoke to me and then continued with their conversation as they went on down the hall. Just as I pushed the elevator button, Noah glanced back over his shoulder and yelled, "Say, how are things going?"

"Just fine," I replied.

They turned and walked back to where I was standing. "Incidentally, you know T. I. Varney, don't you?"

"No, I haven't met him, but I have heard a great deal about him."

Varney was standing with his coat pulled back over his holster, and I could see the edge of his .38 revolver. He stood about five feet six inches tall and was in his late forties, his age lines prominent.

Noah continued, "T. I. is a good man and does a good job in representing the county as a member of the House of Delegates. Anyway, I thought it would be a good idea for you to know each other."

"Perry," said Varney, "I am glad to know you, and I am sure we can work together. I understand everything is coming along fine with this poverty program."

Without hesitation, I replied, "Yes."

"Now you know we will have no trouble working together," Floyd said, "and if you ever need any help, or if I can do anything for you in Charleston, let me know. If we work together, we ought to be able to bring a lot of money into the county. And Johnson wants to give it away. Now I don't know whether you can do anything for these poor people or not. You know most of them are so lazy they won't work. Anyway, keep them happy; we'll need them on election day."

2

Although I had lived in Appalachia all my life, I was stunned by the conditions that I saw during the initial weeks of looking into the hollows of Mingo. The visible effects of poverty were everywhere—the shacks, the filth, the pale, pot-bellied babies, the miners with silicosis, coughing and gasping for breath, the out-houses, the dirt roads, and the one-room schools. Up and down the hollows, the front yards were strewn with junked cars, and the seats from the abandoned automobiles were used for beds and sofas.

Fifty per cent of the county's inhabitants were poor; 20 per cent were welfare recipients; and the unemployment rate was 14 per cent. The remainder of the county's poor were the elderly, most of whom were receiving either Social Security or miners' welfare benefits. Fifty per cent of the homes were substandard. As a result of the leaky roofs, gaping holes, and inadequate heat, infant mortality, usually as a result of pneumonia, was fantastically high compared to the national average.

The people were powerless to counteract the avalanche of individual and community problems inflicted upon them by the selfish economic system that had been organized to remove the coal and timber, leaving the area devoid of wealth. They had also fallen prey to a vicious welfare system that tended to frustrate them with its rules and regulations—imposed by middle class investigators and case workers with less compassion than commitment to the political *status quo*. Adding to the problem was the fact that Mingo's middle class went to great lengths to hide the injustices inflicted on the poor. Many claimed that there was no poverty in the county.

In my own mind, the task before us was clearly defined, and the idea of organized community groups became more appealing day by day. Since Floyd had indicated a general willingness to cooperate, I decided that we might as well take advantage of any assistance that he might be able to offer, regardless of his motives.

Manpower was the initial problem. I knew that, if our plan was to work, we had to reach as many of the poor as possible and as fast as possible. The only available source was the AFDCU enrollees assigned to what everybody called "the State Road." I talked with Floyd and explained that we must make a survey before we could begin to develop federally funded programs. I also said that I would like to borrow at least thirty AFDCU enrollees from the State Road. He gave me an affirmative answer without any hesitation and said that he would call the commissioner of welfare and tell him what we were going to do. Within a week, the welfare department had transferred thirty men to our agency for a three-month period, and, after two days of informal training, the men began their assignments. They were to tell the poor about the new poverty program and invite them to attend community meetings.

14

After several days in the field, we called the first community meeting for a black community known as Vinson Street—actually a hollow located within the Williamson city limits.

I had felt that it would be wise to invite Floyd to the first meeting, primarily to expose him to the ideas of community action and then to observe his response. He came about fifteen minutes before the meeting began, and I had an opportunity to introduce him to Ed Safford and Allen Templeton, who worked for the Council of the Southern Mountains and who had traveled from Berea, Kentucky, for the meeting. The Council, funded by the OEO to provide technical assistance to poverty agencies in West Virginia, Kentucky, and North Carolina, was attempting, as we were, to develop a basic direction for community action. Ed had been a newspaper reporter for a Washington paper, and Allen had just graduated from college. Floyd responded to the introduction by explaining that he was a member of the state Senate and chairman of the Democratic Party in the county. He also said that the EOC had made a fine selection when I had been hired as director.

Jerry Chafin missed the meeting. He was conducting a funeral the following morning and had to stay at the chapel, which was located in his huge two-story funeral home, while the friends and relatives of the deceased attended services.

I was rather amazed at the initial response of the community, for more than seventy residents came to the meeting in Liberty High School, the county's only all-black school, and was quite nervous at the beginning of the meeting. I spent the first few minutes giving the people information about the Economic Opportunity Act, the office in

Washington established by it, and Mingo County's own Economic Opportunity Commission. The community residents appeared to be willing to organize, and they set another meeting date to elect officers. Floyd sat about halfway back in the room, next to the blackboard, and appeared to be very bored during most of the proceedings. He left immediately after the two-hour session.

The following morning, Chafin, dressed in a dark blue suit and derby hat, came to the office. He had only a few minutes to spare before the funeral. "How did the meeting go last night?" he asked.

I replied, "Fairly well; there were about seventy residents. Floyd attended the meeting."

"Incidentally, Huey, I have heard it rumored that something is brewing at Road Branch. You haven't had a meeting there yet, have you?"

"No, we haven't," I told him, "but the organizers have worked the area, and their first meeting is scheduled tonight. I plan to go down. What have you heard?"

"Just heard that some of the people were down looking at the schoolhouse yesterday. That's all."

He took out his pipe and walked to the wastebasket, carefully filling the pipe over it with tobacco from the leather pouch he always carried. Then, walking back to the center of the room, he said, "I would like to go to the meeting tonight, but our lodge is having a meeting, and I am the Grand Master this year; so that has to come first. Anyway, you can tell me what's going on."

I later learned that Chafin belonged to almost every organization in the county and, at one time or another, he had been an officer in each. This was not unusual. As a funeral director, he had a considerable amount of spare time. Before he left, he said, "Better get as much publicity in the newspaper as possible, and, if you write the release, don't forget to mention my name." At first, I thought he was joking, but he was serious. I walked down the hallway with him to the elevator and told him that I would keep him informed about the meeting at Road Branch.

He smiled and said, "I'll see you sometime tomorrow."

I spent most of the day in the office. Jimmy called in several times and said that everything looked good for the meeting at Road Branch. We planned to meet at the school around 6:30 P.M. Later that day, I received a call from the OEO in Washington, inviting Chafin and me to attend a workshop on community action in three weeks. The OEO field analyst assigned to monitor our program, Carolyn Worrell, a West Virginia girl, was interested in our use of AFDCU enrollees as community organizers and wanted me to appear on one of the panels to explain our methods.

I drove to Road Branch earlier than I had previously anticipated and met Jimmy about halfway up the hollow. He was talking with Oliver Spradling, who was cutting weeds for the State Road as an AFDCU worker. Jimmy's shirt was hanging out over his belt in the back, and his collar was soaked with perspiration. I greeted Jimmy, and he introduced me to Spradling.

"I tell you, Perry, these people sure have a lot of complaints," Jimmy said.

"That's right," Spradling intervened. "Them politicians in Williamson won't let me do any work here on this road. Just look at it. You can't hardly get a car over it. Me and some of the fellers up here on the holler asked our boss, Ike Newsome, if we could work up here rather than on the main highway, and he said, 'Hell no! You'll work where I tell you, and, if you don't like it, you can go to hell!' We went to see Johnny Owens, the State Road boss up there in Williamson, and he told us there wasn't anything he could do, that we worked for Ike."

Spradling went on to tell me that he had worked in the mines for twenty-one years, until they closed, and that he had eight children, whom he could hardly support on $165 a month. Three of his children attended the Road Branch grade school at the mouth of the hollow. They had to walk more than a mile a day, even in the winter, for there was no bus service up the narrow hollow road.

There were about thirty people at the meeting. The room was very hot, and the smell of perspiration added to the discomfort. I started the meeting in much the same manner as I had started the one the night before, and, after I explained that we were there to listen to the people's problems, Spradling was fast to take the floor and again go over his encounter with Ike Newsome concerning the road. After about twenty minutes of discussion, Lee Baisden, an elderly ex–coal miner, stood up in the back of the room and said, "Why don't we do like the union used to do? Let's get organized and send a committee to see Johnny Owens, and, if he don't fix the road until a school bus can get over it, by God, I say let's keep our kids out of school."

There was applause, and then Martha Maynard, the wife of an AFDCU enrollee, added, "We'd better get us another committee to go to the Board of Education. Just look at this building. There ain't nary a screen over them windows, and the flies swarm in here like a bee hive. There ain't no drinking water that's fit to drink, and the porch has rotted off."

"And what about the little girl who fell through the outhouse last spring, and that board ain't never sent a crew down here to fix it," Oliver Spradling added.

All over the room, several of the residents were now talking, and it was difficult to hear what anyone was saying. Seeing that the meeting had got out of control, Spradling assumed the role of chairman and asked the crowd to calm down. "We have all recognized our problem; so now let's appoint two committees, one to see the State Road and the other to see the Board of Education," he said.

Baisden replied, "Well, let's just send one committee, and they can stop at both places. Who will volunteer?"

It was finally decided that five volunteers would go, and three men and two women were selected.

The following morning, the committee visited Superintendent of Schools J. Hershel Morgan. Morgan, who was in his early fifties, had come to Mingo from the neighboring county of McDowell. He had a firm grip over the elected school board members and told them only what he wanted them to know. A sergeant during World War II, he had the school system fairly well regimented in an almost military manner.

Morgan arrived at his office, which was air-conditioned but smelled, as always, of cigars, at 9:15. He complained that the group waiting to see him should have made an appointment, and he told them that, if they were to see him in the future, it would be only by appointment. It was almost 11:00 before he invited them in. The spokesman for the committee immediately went over the list of grievances outlined by the community action group.

Morgan's only reply was "Leave the list with me, and I will check it out soon."

Two weeks passed, and no effort was made to respond to

the group's demands. Morgan apparently assumed that this was just another committee. People from other communities had made similar visits in the past and usually without results. What Morgan did not know was that this committee represented a community action group and that it meant business.

After a second visit to the superintendent's office, the group submitted a petition demanding that the school be repaired and stating that the parents would withdraw their children if work did not begin within two days. This demand brought a different reaction from Morgan. It also brought a reaction from the local newspapers. That evening, a brief article appeared on the front page: "Pupil Strike Threatened by Road Branch Community Action Group." According to the committee, Morgan had told them that its members could be put in jail if they called a school strike and had read to them the section of the state law that related to such an act.

The following afternoon, I received a phone call from Paul Crabtree, Governor Hulett Smith's administrative assistant. When the secretary told me who was calling, I was somewhat surprised and could not at first imagine why he would be calling me.

After introducing himself, Crabtree said, "What's this I hear about a pupil strike in Mingo?"

I explained what had happened and what the condition of the school was. I also told him that I thought the community group was justified in its action.

"Don't you know you could be arrested for causing a pupil strike?" he demanded.

"Mr. Crabtree, you had better listen carefully," I said. I was very angry. "I did not call the school strike; it was the parents at Road Branch. And our agency in no way will ever tell a group of people they can't do something when they are damn well justified in doing it."

Crabtree was now more upset than when he first called, and his voice trembled. "I'll tell you, Perry, the governor is not going to like it." He went on to explain that the poverty program was new and that he had been charged to oversee it in the state. "I just don't want to see everything get messed up before it gets started."

"I am sorry that you feel this way," I answered. "There is not a thing I intend to do to stop it."

What I didn't tell Crabtree was that, if I did anything, I would continue to encourage the community in its efforts. This battle was an important one for community action in Mingo. If the people lost, it would be difficult to get them to act again on any matter. If they won, their action could be used as an example before other groups.

Fortunately for community action, the Board of Education sent in a maintenance crew the following day. The schoolhouse was painted; the porch and the outhouses were repaired; screens were placed in the windows; a flagpole was erected; and paper cups replaced the thirteen glasses that had previously been shared by forty-three students.

The local paper carried the story: "Board Meets the Demands of the Road Branch Group." This was a major victory for community action, and the story was told before every group in Mingo County and used as an example of what group action could achieve.

3

Jimmy and I arrived early for the meeting at Goodman, a small mining community about twelve miles west of Williamson. He and several AFDCU enrollees had been working the area for several days and felt the time was right for organizing the community.

I drove up the hollow known as Dan's Branch, just to get a look at the physical setting before the meeting, and on the way up I noticed several people walking out to the mouth of the hollow. The meeting was to be held in an old coal company building. Jimmy pointed out a house high on the side of a mountain where a snake-handling preacher lived. As far as I know, he was the only snake-handling preacher in the county, and I was hoping that he would leave his religion at home if he came to the meeting. Thinking about trying to explain the concept of community action with a copperhead crawling down the aisle, I told Jimmy that I could stand the politicians at a meeting but not the snakes.

Forty-six residents of Goodman turned out to hear us explain the role of the Economic Opportunity Commission and the purpose of our meeting. Everyone listened intently, and then several talked about the housing problem. Others told of their own individual hardships and the troubles they had with the local welfare department.

Ira Phillips, an AFDCU enrollee assigned to cut weeds on the state highway, said, "You just can't get a thing out of that welfare department lessen you vote for Noah Floyd's gang, and then it's so little you can't get by on it."

The snake-handling preacher and his wife sat near the back of the room, listening to the discussion. Noticing his silence, I asked whether he would be interested in helping to organize a community action group in the area. He rose to his feet, walked over to a window, raised it, and spat his tobacco out. Turning toward the group, he said, "I'll tell you, brothers and sisters that are gathered here tonight, there is only one kind of organization I will help organize, and that is the church of the living God."

His voice grew louder and faster as he proceeded. "I'll tell you there is too much wickedness in this here world for me to worry about worldly things, and the only way out is the way of the Lord. The Lord said if you will believe in him that he'll take care of you, and, if you don't believe, you will be condemned to hellfire and damnation. And, brothers and sisters, the flames of hell are hot.

"Who knows among us who has sent these government men in here to organize us and get us to accept things of the world. For all we know, they may be communist. The Lord saith the poor shall inherit the kingdom of God, and in Revelation he also speaks of the mark of the beast. In the last day, everyone who signs up will have a mark on his forehead and a number in the palm of his hand. And, brothers and sisters, who is to say this ain't the mark of the beast?"

23

An elderly lady in the second row said, "Amen." Another shouted, "Amen, brother; let the spirit of the Lord speak out!"

He smiled and gazed at the crowd. "Now just look at you back there, Jed. You ain't never attended a one of my church services, and, besides that, you ain't worked a day in the last ten years, not since the mine closed down. But you are the first in line when you hear of a handout.

"Oh God, oh God," he shouted as he pounded his clenched fist on a seat top, "what is this world coming to? My brothers and sisters, let me tell you here, now, and forever, if you don't believe in God, there ain't nothing that can be done for you. And, brother, let me tell you there are scriptures in the New Testament that clearly show the way. It's easier for the camel to pass through the eye of a needle than it is for a rich man to enter the kingdom of heaven."

He slowed his pace. "Now I've told you what I think, and me and my wife are going home, and, brothers, we shall pray for you."

This was our first confrontation with religious fundamentalism at one of our meetings. It was apparent from the preacher's remarks that he felt it better to remain poor, that one's chances of going to heaven increased in proportion to one's degree of poverty. How widespread this belief was in Mingo was hard to determine, but it was evident that it had supporters in Goodman. Several people walked out with the preacher and his wife.

After our failure to organize the Goodman group, we focused our attention on the community of Vulcan, at the opposite end of the county. Vulcan had been at one time a thriving mining community. But, as in other communities, the mine had long been closed, leaving behind a half-empty coal camp. Only thirty families remained. Their biggest problem was that the state had forgotten to build a road into the community. Although state maps showed a road into Vulcan, it was nowhere to be found. The only way people could get in and out was to drive up the Kentucky side and walk across a swinging bridge, which was too narrow for a vehicle. The bridge had been built by the coal company years before and was on the verge of collapse; although there were boards missing, the children had to walk across it to catch the school bus on the Kentucky side.

The Vulcan group had met twice and had elected Troy Blankenship as chairman. Troy operated a barbershop and grocery store, the only business in Vulcan. He was a very outspoken individual and was always complaining about the dirty politics in Mingo. Troy's left leg was off just above the knee. He had lost it when he was eleven years old, as he crawled under a coal car that was parked on a siding. The railroad still uses that same siding to park loaded coal cars, and the children still crawl under them to get to the one-room elementary school, which is located just opposite the tracks and adjacent to Troy's store.

The missing road and the bad bridge had been the Vulcan group's chief complaints at the first two community meetings, and someone had suggested that someone should write to Congressman Jim Kee concerning the problems. Kee had always been an astute politician, avoiding any controversy, always able to stay in the middle. The inquiry from the group was answered promptly. He suggested they invite several public agencies, from both the state and federal governments, along with officials from the N & W Railroad, which owned most of the property at Vulcan, to discuss the problems and to determine whether any solutions were possible.

The group accepted the suggestion and decided to invite representatives from the Office of Economic Opportunity, the Department of Health, Education, and Welfare, and the U.S. Department of Labor, along with their state counterparts and the State Road Commission. Within a few days, all the agencies invited agreed to send representatives. In addition, the county politicians had been invited.

The evening of this third meeting, I drove to Vulcan with Ben McDonald, our field representative from the OEO office in Washington. Before taking the OEO job, he had been pastor of a Presbyterian church in the Washington suburbs. He was full of questions concerning our approach to community organization. I attempted to bring him up to date concerning the local power structure and explained that the local politicians would be present that night. Congressman Kee had sent Frank Tsutras, his administrative assistant, down for the meeting.

At 6:30, the N & W passenger train made an unusual stop at Vulcan. Three officials from the company stepped down from the last coach. Two were carrying brief cases. Already the residents of Vulcan were gathering at the schoolhouse. They were just standing around, eying the many strangers who were arriving. Tsutras had brought most of the federal officials with him from Williamson. He and several of them were observing the swinging bridge that crossed the Tug River.

I was talking with William Mounts, a disabled coal miner who had been severely crippled in a slate fall in the mines in the late 1950's. He had been paralyzed for several

26

months but had fought back bravely and could now walk on crutches. He was telling me that he also had silicosis from the coal dust in the mines and had a hard time breathing. Troy Blankenship came over to where we were talking. He was dressed in his black suit and black tie, and appeared a little nervous. "Mr. Perry," he asked, "do you think I should conduct the meeting?"

"Certainly," I said. "The people have elected you chairman of the group, and that is part of your job."

Several children, many with dirty faces and torn clothes, were running back and forth through the schoolyard, and many of the community women were inside preparing coffee and cookies to be served at the end of the meeting.

Troy yelled at one of the women, "Mrs. Felty, come here," and, when she did, said, "I would like for you to meet Mr. Perry. He's the director of this new poverty program in Williamson."

Louise Felty smiled. "Well, I'll declare, I thought you were an older man. I figured it would take an older man to do a job like you have."

Troy explained that Mrs. Felty had taught school at Vulcan for the past fifteen years.

"I'll tell you, Mr. Perry," she said, "we sure need a road here into this community. Some of these kids are going to get killed on that bridge. If you came across it, you noticed there are several boards missing."

When the meeting was finally convened, the large school room was unable to hold everyone, and several stood outside in the hall. Several people from Kentucky had come, just out of curiosity. Troy seated all the guests in the front and called the meeting to order.

"Now, I am not much of a speaker," he said, as his voice

faltered and his face became flushed, "but let me tell you one thing, we have got to have a road here in Vulcan. Before I get started, let me introduce our guests." One by one, he introduced the front row and, most of the time, mispronounced their names, and he almost forgot to introduce the county officials, who were sitting in the audience. He was more interested in telling the guests about Vulcan's problem than in letting people know who they were.

"First of all, we went to Williamson and tried to talk with that bunch down there," he said, obviously making a reference to the local politicians, "and they promised they would do something for this bridge. That's been three years ago. But let me tell you, when it comes time for election again, we are going to remember. We are plumb fed up with you politicians!" He was looking straight at Steve Adkins, the sheriff. "The only thing you are interested in is what money you can make from the people."

Rumors were widespread throughout the county that the sheriff was collecting twenty-five to fifty dollars a month from all the beer establishments in the county. This contribution gave them the right to operate an illicit business. Those who refused to pay were closed down or raided so often that they went bankrupt. Steve turned a little red in the face but did not comment.

Troy continued for fifteen or twenty minutes, blasting the local politicians, and he did not spare any words. He then started on the N & W Railroad, recalling in detail the time he lost his leg, and he asked directly why the N & W would not allow the community to use the side road adjacent to the main line. From Delorme, a small community five miles below Vulcan, the railroad company had a road built in order to transport maintenance men by truck. However, the company had erected a "No Trespassing" sign and had the road blocked with chains at both ends. Several of the community people had been arrested for using the road to haul coal during the winter months. Each time, the justice of the peace had fined them $17.50 for trespassing.

One of the N & W officials replied that the road was too dangerous for cars to use. Besides, he said, it would jeopardize the railroad, and the railroad would be responsible if an accident occurred. "Do you realize what one train wreck would cost the company? I can tell you it would cost more than this whole community is worth, twenty times over." As he sat down, he said, "I am sorry, the N & W is unable to help you. We feel it is a problem for the county and state."

There was silence in the room. Before the meeting, the best hope had seemed to be the access road owned by the N & W. The N & W official had just dimmed the hopes of the people of Vulcan.

It was apparent that Troy was disgusted. He turned to the representative of the State Road Commission and asked him whether he had anything to say.

The well-dressed man in his early thirties, who identified himself as an engineer for the State Road Commission, had come well prepared with maps and statistics concerning economic feasibility. He began, "First, I would like to say the governor, Hulett Smith, is deeply concerned about the plight of you people here. Unfortunately, this area of the state is a low priority area, and it is not economically feasible to construct a highway into Vulcan from Delorme. The total cost would involve 6 million dollars. This cost is due to the high cliffs behind the railroad. We have looked at other possible routes, and they, too, are out of the cost ratio."

Troy interrupted, "If that is all you came from Charleston to tell us, you have wasted your time and ours, too. You are all just a bunch of politicians and no better than the ones in Williamson."

At this point, Frank Tsutras, feeling somewhat embarrassed by Troy and many of the comments that were coming from the other people, decided to make a statement. "I am Frank Tsutras, administrative assistant to Jim Kee. The good congressman has asked me to apologize for him not being here. His wife was sick, and he was unable to leave Washington. We have had a great deal of discussion here tonight without reaching any conclusions. I believe we can solve this problem. Maybe it will take additional engineering studies, and perhaps we can secure some money from the Appalachian Regional Commission."

Frank rambled on for several more minutes, every now and then putting in a word for the "hardworking congressman," as he described Jim Kee.

In the back of the room, one man mumbled to a friend, "The old son of a bitch is probably up in Washington, drunk as usual. The only goddamn thing he has ever been concerned with is winning an election."

"Yeah, he's tied right in with that gang in the courthouse. Troy ain't going to get a damn thing out of this meeting but a big bunch of promises, and, the way it looks, he ain't even going to get a good promise."

"That damn Kee ain't fitten to be a congressman. If it hadn't been for his daddy and mommy, he couldn't even got elected to the state legislature."

The meeting had been going on for about an hour and forty minutes when Tsutras sat down.

Troy said, "Well, Mr. Tsutras, you haven't been much

of a help either. I want to say to you people, we are not going to give up our fight for a way in and out of Vulcan. Now, I know not much was accomplished here tonight, but I don't guess we expected much to happen—just the same old stories we have always heard. There's coffee and cookies in the next room; so all of you go in there and get yourselves something to eat."

The crowd slowly dispersed, and several went home. Others moved into the other room for refreshments, and there, among the people of Vulcan who stayed, could be overheard more disgruntled statements concerning the meeting and local politicians—especially Noah Floyd, for they knew that he controlled everything in the county.

Before the refreshments were all gone, Troy announced that he intended to go to Washington if the community would help finance the trip. The sheriff, Steve Adkins, whispered to Larry Hamrick, who had just joined the EOC staff as assistant director, "That Troy is crazy as hell!"

4

At the end of eight months, Jimmy and Larry Hamrick and I had organized twenty-six community action groups throughout the county. (Not long after, Jimmy left the EOC to go back to the country music business.) Many of the groups were involved with such projects as fencing a community cemetery or developing a small recreational area. Several were making demands upon the Mingo County Board of Education to extend school bus services farther up the hollows or to build small roadside shelters for the children to stand in while waiting for their bus. Others were sending to the State Road Commission delegations demanding better roads up the hollows.

Both the Board of Education and the Road Commission were reacting favorably, and, in many instances, hollow roads were graveled and school bus services improved. It was evident that both groups wanted to avoid another confrontation with the people like the one the Board of Education had encountered with the Road Branch group.

Practically every community group feared the local politicians, but many of the poor were beginning to speak out against the school board and Noah Floyd. Participation in a community group afforded them security for the first time in their lives. More and more, they were describing and complaining openly about the injustices of the welfare department and Noah's control of the recipients of checks and the transfer of AFDCU enrollees to undesirable jobs if they failed to obey his commands.

By now, it was becoming an increasingly difficult task to defend community organization to the Board of Directors of the EOC, which was primarily made up of members of the county's established institutions. We were getting inquiries daily regarding the activities of the community groups.

At a Commission meeting, O. T. Kent, representing the Board of Education, rose to his feet and asked for recognition: "Mr. Chairman, may I say a few words? It has come to my attention that many of those so-called poor people have been coming into the Board of Education office and demanding that Mr. Morgan do such and such. They are not asking; they are demanding. Now I think there is a right way and a wrong way for people to act. When I want to see someone in authority, I always call for an appointment, and I don't demand; I ask." (Kent, a man in his late sixties, worked as a land agent for the Cotega Development Company, one of the largest absentee landowners in the county.) "I think it is outrageous the way those people carried on down at Road Branch a few months ago. Every one of them could have been put in jail for threatening a school strike, and we've had groups from Browning Fork and Big Branch wanting school buses run farther up the hollows. For example, in order just to satisfy them over at Browning Fork, we are running the school bus an extra

33

mile just to pick up three kids. I'll tell you one thing, it won't hurt people to have a few hardships. I had them when I was growing up. Our whole family had to work. People have got to want to help themselves. Now, we've been doing a lot of things these groups have been wanting done, and mainly we don't want them to embarrass the county like the Road Branch group did. Anyway, I think, Mr. Chairman, that you should instruct Mr. Perry there to calm these people down and tell them what they can have and what they can't have."

As Kent sat down, several of the EOC board members nodded in approval of what he had said. Many of the people against whom he was directing his criticisms were standing in the back of the room observing the meeting. They had no voice on the Commission but were listening very intently to Kent, for the first time hearing an elected official express discontent with many of their groups' actions.

Chafin asked me whether I would explain to Kent the function of the community action groups. I rose to my feet and explained once again the Economic Opportunity Act, placing special emphasis on "maximum feasible involvement of the poor."

Kent was very attentive as I said, "They are organized for the purpose of identifying community problems and then seeking a solution. We are obligated to provide assistance to the groups in solving their problems." I was quite evasive with the remainder of my explanation. I knew the time was not right for a showdown with the Commission regarding the direction community action would take in Mingo. If the Board of Directors knew we had encouraged the poor at Road Branch and Browning Fork to take the

34

actions they took, we would be dismissed immediately.

Next, there were questions concerning the Vulcan meeting. Several of the Commission members stated that they had heard a number of rumors concerning the meeting and that Troy Blankenship had used it to embarrass the politicians. I did not attempt to give an explanation for Troy's behavior.

When a retired coal miner in the back of the room, Clyde Robinette, asked for permission to speak, he was told by Chafin that he would have to wait until after the meeting was over, because he was not a member of the Board of Directors.

Robinette became angry. "I thought, Mr. Chafin, that this poverty program was for the poor, and why don't we have a right to say what's on our mind?"

Chafin rapped the table for order. "Mr. Robinette, I will have to declare you out of order."

Although it was difficult to restrain myself, I felt it better to keep quiet. Robinette was perfectly correct and should have had the privilege of speaking. He told me later he was waiting to reply to O. T. Kent's statement. Clyde lived at Road Branch and had five children in school.

During the same meeting, Chafin announced that the EOC had received $150,000 from the Department of Labor to operate a Neighborhood Youth Corps (NYC) program for the in-school children of low income families. The students would work two hours a day and earn $1.25 per hour.

It had been the strategy of the staff to get this program developed primarily to bring some federal money into the county to keep the Board of Directors happy. Its concept of a successful poverty program was determined by the amount of federal dollars that could be brought into the county. If additional money would appease the EOC directors, then it would give us time to organize the poor so that they could have a genuine voice in developing the types of programs that would best serve their needs.

Chafin announced that the agency would be hiring a director for the NYC program and appointed an interviewing committee. It was made up from practically the same group that had interviewed me. Evidently the word got back quickly to Noah that a staff position was open, for he came to my office early the next morning.

Chewing on a cigar, he came directly into my office without asking Donna, the EOC secretary, whether I was in. "Hi there, Perry. How are things going?"

"Fine," I replied.

"Say, I heard you were looking for a new person," and without hesitation, "I've got just the man you need, Tony Gentile."

Tony had been football coach at Williamson High School and had dabbled in local politics practically all of his life. He had been elected to the state legislature, but Noah's machine had failed to support him during the last election, and he was badly beaten by T. I. Varney. To the poor, he was just another politician, and, in private conversations with many of the local community leaders, I had been highly critical of the politicians. If we were to hire Tony Gentile, it would be the end of the poverty program.

I explained to Noah that the EOC board had selected an interviewing committee that would consider applications within five days.

"Do you have the applications here?" he asked.

I replied, "Yes," and gave him one.

He continued. "Now, the reason I want to hire Tony is,

36

simply, I want to get him off my back. There is a rumor going around that he plans to run against me next time. Now, I am not concerned about him beating me, but I would prefer not to have any opposition. Besides, he has a lot of Jewish friends here in Williamson, and it would help the party. There are a lot of them mad because I didn't support him the last time, but he was developing too much power, and I was afraid he would double-cross me.

"I tell you what: You keep the application here, and I'll send Tony up this afternoon and have him fill it out. You can call Gerald Chafin and tell him I want Tony."

Noah left, and I sat there in utter confusion as to what to do about the situation. Finally, I called Richard Cutlip, who was chairman of the committee, and told him of Noah's request. Richard had been going to several community action meetings with me, and he was the one person on the Board of Directors whom I could trust. But he had to be very careful also, because Noah had a great deal of influence with West Virginia University, where Richard taught, and could have him moved from the county. He had told me of an incident in which his secretary had lost her job when she refused to contribute $10 a month to Noah's fund. The County Court paid her salary and, after she refused to contribute, found an excuse to withhold it, thus leaving her no choice but to resign. Richard was still angry about the incident, but he had not protested, because he had bought a home in Mingo and didn't want to leave.

He was in full agreement with me about Tony and felt that hiring him would certainly create mistrust of the agency. He said that he would discuss the matter with one or two of the other committee members and get their opin-

37

ion. In the meantime, we sought other applications. Five people applied for the job—all schoolteachers. On the evening of the interviews, I met with the committee and openly voiced my opposition to Gentile. Cutlip did the same thing, and, fortunately, Gentile was not hired.

Cutlip and I both feared that our opposition to Gentile would get back to Noah. But, as it happened, Noah blamed Gerald Chafin. He felt that Chafin, as chairman of the board, could have used his influence to get Tony the job.

Noah didn't visit the office during the next two weeks. My next contact with him came in the dining room of the Mountaineer Hotel, where most of the politicians, lawyers, and office workers ate. He was sitting with Sheriff Steve Adkins at a table facing the entrance and waved for Larry and me to join them. We pulled chairs up to their table and sat down. Noah seemed friendly enough. He didn't mention the Gentile incident, but said he had been to Washington with a delegation from the local Chamber of Commerce to secure funds for a local airport construction project. We chatted a few minutes after lunch, and he insisted on paying the bill, assuring Larry and me that he would do anything he could to help us. After they left, Larry and I sat bewildered, for we had not expected Floyd to forget so easily the fact that he had failed to get Gentile hired. Nevertheless, we felt relieved that he was not angry.

We went back to the office at 1:30 P.M. Donna informed me that Ben McDonald, our field representative, had called from Washington and wanted me to return his call, which was very urgent. When I got Ben on the phone, I could hear the anxiety in his voice.

"What the hell was that delegation doing up here yesterday from Williamson?" he asked.

"What do you mean? At the OEO office?" I questioned.

"No, they weren't here but over at Senator Byrd's office," he replied.

"Oh, don't worry about that. It was Noah Floyd, the county chairman, Howard Coleman, Chamber of Commerce president, and Sid Copley, director of the Chamber of Commerce, plus a few others, who were up there talking with Byrd about getting money to construct an airport in Mingo. How did you know they were up there?"

He replied, somewhat puzzled, "I don't understand it. I just got a call from Byrd's assistant, asking me to come to his office as soon as possible. He didn't say what it was about other than he wanted to discuss a request made by a delegation from Williamson, Mingo County. Okay, I am going over there now, and I will call you back if it means anything."

"Fine, Ben. I'll be in the office late, so be sure to call me."

At 6:00 P.M., Ben called back. "Huey, I've got serious news. You are going to be investigated."

"What the hell are you talking about, Ben?"

"I am serious. That delegation from Mingo was evidently not up here for airport funds at all. They have asked Byrd to investigate the EOC because you are supposedly involved in political activity."

"Why, those dirty sons of bitches!" I shouted. Then I proceeded to tell Ben about having lunch with Noah and the fact that he had not given the slightest indication that he was disturbed.

Ben explained, "Actually, what will happen is this. The regional office will request someone from OEO headquarters inspection staff to come down and check out the com-

39

plaints. As an analyst, I haven't been through this before. Anyway, I am sure you will come through with flying colors."

Once Ben was off the phone, I discussed the entire situation with Larry, and together we drafted an immediate news release for the local paper. We felt that it was best to let the public know what was taking place, and, besides, it appeared that the agency had nothing to lose. Apparently, this was Floyd's way of getting even. Floyd was blaming Chafin for not hiring Gentile, and Chafin was somewhat angry with Floyd. We decided to try to take advantage of the opportunity to completely divide Floyd and Chafin by persuading Chafin to release the news article.

I called Chafin and explained in detail what had happened, and convinced him that Noah had to be stopped. He agreed to be quoted in a news release, which he presented the following morning to the local daily paper. It read, in part:

> The recent trip to Washington made by Noah Floyd, Mingo County State Senator; Howard Coleman, president of the Tug Valley Chamber of Commerce; and Sidney Copley, Chamber director, in addition to inquiring into further feasibility of an airport for Mingo, also asked to have the activities of the Mingo County E.O.C. investigated.
>
> During a conference with U. S. Senator Robert Byrd, the men made the request. This information was confirmed by Sidney Copley in a telephone conversation with me.
>
> These representatives feel that the Mingo E.O.C., through its 26 community action groups, are attempting to set up a political machine, and they indicated they had heard such rumors.
>
> I am completely surprised by the action of these men, and it appears to be an attempt by county politicians to take over the E.O.C. and, like everything else, make it a political foot-

ball, and use it to hand out jobs to political friends, instead of helping the poor people of the county.

On numerous occasions, certain politicians have approached me in regard to placing certain people on the E.O.C. staff. Not a member of the staff has ever been hired as a result of politics.

I can point with pride to the E.O.C. record and to the fact that 26 communities have action groups, making an effort to better themselves. . . .

As long as I am president of the Mingo E.O.C., no politician will ever dictate policies. If politics gets in, it is doomed and the poor will suffer.

The following day, Howard Coleman, president of the Chamber of Commerce, released a statement in retaliation to the Chafin article, saying, in part:

Many reports have come to me recently concerning controversies between the school board and other school officials and the Mingo County Economic Opportunity Commission officials. All of these reports had political overtones.

Feeling that a continuation of these reports would not be in the best interest of Mingo County, and after having discussed this with many people, the general thinking was that these reports should be called to the attention of top O.E.O. officials. After discussing this situation with Senator Byrd on his recent visit, it was suggested that a conference be held with these officials.

This conference was arranged and held when I was in Washington earlier this week with a local group there in the interest of the Mingo County airport.

This conference was told of the reports, and the O.E.O. officials were asked to make a confidential investigation to determine for themselves conditions as they exist. They were asked to do this without publicity. Also, I told them that this investigation should be done before the school board election and that if political activities were involved, that corrective measures should be made immediately.

No accusations were made against any particular person in this ten to fifteen minute conference.

Tom Kelly from the OEO Inspection Office visited Mingo the following week. After talking with several community people and political leaders, he came to our office.

Tom indicated that the school administrators were upset because Head Start funds had been channeled through the EOC, which gave the antipoverty agency final authority in decisions that affected the program. The greatest conflict resulted when the antipoverty agency insisted that teachers' aides be hired from among the mothers of the Head Start children. School administrators viewed this as an absolute insult to the teaching profession in Mingo County. One irate teacher had said to Tom, "That EOC bunch is crazy. Teaching is a professional job, and they think you can take a welfare recipient and make a teacher out of her, when, in fact, the welfare people are the ones that cause all the problems."

Because the school officials had taken such a harsh attitude regarding the use of welfare mothers as teachers' aides, many of the citizens involved in community action had begun to criticize the school system. This criticism had been interpreted by the members of the Board of Education to mean that the EOC was becoming politically involved in the upcoming Board of Education election.

Tom concluded that he had found no evidence of people employed by the agency participating in politics. He pointed out that there were no regulations that prohibited employees from participating in nonpartisan elections such as the school board election. He said that the report would be made public and that we would be cleared of all charges.

5

When we began to develop and write the programs for the second fiscal year of Mingo County's War on Poverty, the initial grant received from the OEO for program development was almost exhausted. The two priorities that had been established by the community action groups were community organization and home improvement. Once the programs were written, we requested only $108,000 for both priorities, and that amount also included funds for the administration of the agency. The amount of federal funds requested was very modest when compared to many community action programs throughout the country, especially in McDowell County.

The community organization component requested seven community organizers to be stationed in seven geographical areas throughout the county to assist the community action groups and to provide a communications link between the people and the agency.

The home improvement program was designed to make emergency repairs on low income homes. It was proposed that the OEO fund eight carpenters and that the local welfare department assign enrolees from its AFDCU program to receive training as carpenters' aides while repairs were being made on substandard houses.

Noah's brother George was the county supervisor for the AFDCU program, and he had assigned 400 of the men to the State Road Commission to cut weeds and clean ditches. Another 150 were assigned to the County Court to dig graves. Each of the magisterial districts had what the people called a "graveyard crew." The only time that these enrollees worked was when someone in that magisterial district died.

The AFDCU program was originally designed to provide a "meaningful and useful work experience." This objective was certainly not attained in Mingo. The assignments were merely an extension of the Democratic political patronage system. The State Road Commission and the County Court also hired work supervisors and assigned fifteen to twenty men to each supervisor. Their primary concern with the men was to force them to vote for the machine slate of candidates on election day. Many of the enrollees were bitterly opposed to the AFDCU program and the way it was operated. But, afraid of losing their checks, they always did what they were told.

After the OEO investigation, the supervisors, fearing that the men would begin speaking out against the program and the county political organization, ordered them to stay away from the community action meetings. This situation was a serious blow to our efforts because these were the poor we were attempting to organize. Including their families, nearly six thousand people were dependent on this program.

The State Commissioner of Welfare, L. L. Vincent, after

44

several meetings, agreed to assign thirty men to our home improvement program. But, each time I discussed the matter with him, he reminded me that he had had a serious problem in the beginning, when we had used AFDCU enrollees to assist with the county survey. He insinuated that the problems came directly from state Senator Noah Floyd.

When the assignments were finally made and the men reported out to work, we discovered to our amazement that seven of the thirty were physically incapable of performing carpentry work. One man had lost his leg in a mining accident, and one had lost his arm. It was difficult to imagine either of these men repairing the roof of a house. The remainder of the group were elderly men who were not interested in such work. George Floyd, the county supervisor, had made the selections. We complained bitterly to one of Vincent's assistants, Jim Framton, and he assured us that the situation would be corrected. It was corrected, but not until three months later.

The community groups, eager to implement the newly funded home improvement program, became very much irritated with the state welfare department and its lack of concern. On two occasions, efforts were made to organize the AFDCU men into an association. But fear of the politicians dominated, and each time the effort ended in failure.

Another failure occurred at Dingess when the local political arm of the Floyd machine won control of the community action group, leaving the poor as powerless as before. The new OEO grant had provided for seven additional staff members to be hired as community organizers. Cletis Blackburn, a disabled World War II veteran, had been assigned the area of Harvey District. He was constantly complaining about how the local politicians in the area were destroying any possibility of creating a viable community group. However, he was determined to change the situation.

One evening, my phone at home rang at 10:30. I had gone to bed early with the expectation of going to Morgantown the next morning to meet with OEO and West Virginia University officials to assist them in the formulation of a training program for the community action agencies in West Virginia. My plane was to leave from the Charleston airport at 7:00 A.M., meaning that I would have to leave home at 4:00 A.M. to make the hundred-mile trip up the narrow, winding roads.

Half-asleep, I answered the phone.

"Is that you, Huey?"

"Yes," I answered.

"This is Hi Marcum at Dingess." He spoke very slowly. "You had better check on your man Cletis Blackburn. I think he is in serious trouble. Della Wellman and her gang of outlaws broke up the meeting tonight and ran everyone off. We are kinda worried about Cletis. Tried to make him stay here with us, but nothing would do him except go on home. He was supposed to call us, but he ain't, and he has had plenty of time to get home."

I did not take time to go into detail with Marcum concerning what had actually taken place. If the people of Dingess were worried, I knew very well that something bad had happened. I immediately placed a call to an EOC community aide who lived only eight miles from Cletis and asked her to drive by Cletis's home to see whether he had returned. Because he had no telephone, there was no other way to reach him. Thirty minutes later, she called back to inform me that Cletis had not returned.

If Cletis was in danger, it would take too long for me to drive to Dingess. I lived fifty miles away. Therefore, I called Jerry Chafin, informed him of the situation, and suggested that he call the state police to investigate. It was 11:15, and he was to call me back as soon as he could learn something of Cletis's whereabouts. At 1:30 A.M., I received a call from Chafin's wife, Marie, who informed me that Jerry had made contact with the state police. Jerry and three carloads of the "States," as they were referred to locally, were on their way into Dingess.

I had known Dingess was a potential trouble spot for community organization, but I had not expected any violence from the opposition. Three months earlier, when the new group was first organized, the Harvey District had been used as a training area for the freshly hired community organizers. Ed Safford and his wife-to-be had come up from Berea College in Kentucky to assist in organizing the community and to conduct the training. He had taken our entire staff into the area and had spent three days talking with the people and inviting them to the first community meeting to be held in the grade school building.

I remember that Ed had come back to the office after the second day, tired but excited, for that afternoon he had met the mother of Blaze Starr, the well-known stripper who had made herself famous in Baltimore. Ed said that the mother had brought out all the pictures she had of Blaze, plus some of two younger daughters who were learning to become strippers, and had spent two hours telling of Blaze's success. It was news to me. I had heard of Blaze Starr but did not know she was from Mingo.

I could tell from Ed's enthusiasm that he was delighted with the people he had met and also amazed by the entire

47

area of Harvey District where the community of Dingess was located. To get into the area, one had to pass through an abandoned railroad tunnel, which was nine-tenths of a mile long. Years ago, the Chesapeake and Ohio (C & O) Railroad came from Huntington up Twelve Pole Creek into Williamson. In the early 1930's, the track was abandoned, and the state then used the old railroad bed for a highway. The road was narrow and followed along Twelve Pole Creek, crossing several one-lane railroad bridges, which had been floored with heavy oak. The bridges were very dangerous because the high steel sides blocked oncoming traffic from view.

At the mouth of Laurel Creek, where the road branches off U.S. Route 52 toward Dingess, the State Road Commission had erected a sign with an arrow pointing, "See the Scenic Dingess Tunnel—9 Miles." For that distance up Laurel Creek toward Dingess, there was a fairly decent road, and the state had provided a small fishing lake and picnic area and, later, a swimming pool near the entrance of the tunnel. Noah Floyd took full credit for the construction of this little park and campaigned on the fact that it had been one of his major accomplishments for the county. The state had also constructed a log cabin on the site, but it was rumored that no one was allowed to use it except Noah and his friends.

The tunnel itself was far from scenic. It was more like a dungeon, as it was once described by a visitor from Florida, who had taken the sign seriously. It was faced with large red bricks, long since covered by green moss, with the exception of the last quarter of a mile, which was constructed of huge cut stones. Streams of water fell profusely from the ceiling. The bottom was dirt and full of holes; maximum

48

speed was ten miles per hour. Upon entering the tunnel, drivers sometimes found it impossible, because of heavy fog, to determine whether another car had already entered from the other end. Time and time again, cars would have to back out of the one-way tunnel.

The most frightening thing about the Dingess tunnel, however, was that three victims of unsolved murders had been found in it. In fact, the entire Harvey District was frightening. Old-timers there said it was common practice to have a killing once a month. As "Uncle" Jim Marcum described it, "Why, a colored person couldn't think about riding through Dingess. They would stop the train, take him off and shoot him, and nobody would say a word. Why, they would even stop the train and take all its cargo. It was a wild country then, and it ain't much better now." Since 1900, seventeen lawmen had been shot to death in the area, which stretches fifteen miles along Twelve Pole Creek and is the poorest section in Mingo County. Over 50 per cent of its three thousand people in the 1960's were dependent on welfare, and the only sign of industry was two small sawmills, which employed about six men each. Unlike other parts of the county, it had no coal mines—not even small truck mines. The shacks were spread far apart up and down the hollows and creeks.

Politically, the Wellman family controlled the area, and almost everyone feared its power. Della Wellman, who, in her late sixties, with her hair combed straight back and twisted into a bun at the back, gave the appearance of being the most powerless woman in the county, was Noah Floyd's mainstay in the community. She had succeeded her late husband as a member of the Democratic executive committee some nineteen years before, when he was shot and killed in an election brawl in the school gymnasium. Her three sons were all employed by the state. One had been shot through the neck and had difficulty with his speech. Della worked as a janitor at the grade school.

When the community action group was first organized at Dingess, Della Wellman, who was commonly known as the "old blue goose," made sure that one of her relatives was elected chairman. She had ordered all the AFDCU enrollees who were assigned to the State Road Commission to attend the meeting. The organizational meeting was held at the Dingess grade school, and I had traveled to Dingess that evening with Ed Safford and Larry Hamrick, the EOC's assistant director. We arrived at the building about fifteen minutes before the scheduled beginning of the meeting and found an enormous crowd of local residents. It was obvious that the training session had been a success as far as getting people out to a meeting was concerned. The meeting lasted for about an hour. I explained the Economic Opportunity Act and the purpose of community organization.

Halfway through the meeting, Della stood up and explained how she, as a member of the Democratic executive committee, would be willing to cooperate and do anything she could for the group. "You all know that I have made every effort possible to help this community. Why, I don't even know how many of you people I got on relief."

At that point, Delphia Meade suggested that Della be elected chairman of the group because she had influence with Floyd in Williamson. She said, "You people know if we are to get anything done for the community that we will have to cooperate with the elected officials."

The crowd was silent, and no one suggested another

nominee for chairman. Della once again rose to her feet, gazed around at the people, and appeared to be extremely pleased that no one had resisted her. "I appreciate you people wanting me as your chairman, but, as you know, I am a very busy person, and I really don't have time for such a job. Anyway, I would like to recommend Maxine Dingess to you, and I am sure she will do a good job. Besides, she is a schoolteacher. I know what everyone needs in this community, and I will stand behind her one hundred per cent."

I was quite concerned with the method that was being used to select a chairman. However, it was clear that Della Wellman was the political power in the community and that she was going to control the group, regardless of who was elected. There was no resistance to her suggesting Maxine, whose election, after Della's recommendation, became automatic.

My other concern was the fact that Della was making the people believe that she was responsible for getting them signed up for welfare and food stamps. Perhaps she was doing a very effective job. The welfare department was extremely political, and I suppose this was one example of the Democratic "referral system" in operation.

On the way back to Williamson, Ed and I talked about the meeting and what had happened. We were both wondering how it would ever be possible to create political independence in a community such as Dingess, where the people were so dependent on an individual like Della. Certainly there was nothing we could have done during the meeting to alter the situation. We concluded that change must be brought about outside the meetings and that it was going to take patience and understanding to influence the attitude of the people.

During the next three months, the crowds grew smaller and smaller, and, finally, there were only seven or eight people attending the meetings. On several occasions, even Maxine didn't bother to attend. It was quite a dilemma for the staff. I had spent several hours with Cletis discussing the lack of interest within the community, and we attempted to develop a strategy. We believed that the primary cause of the lack of interest was the people's dependence on Della Wellman.

Ultimately, we decided to attempt a new experiment with the poor in Dingess and, at the same time, to eliminate Maxine Dingess as chairman. The plan of establishing a neighborhood corporation with a board of directors elected from among the poor would be the first step toward independence. Cletis and I discussed the strategy very thoroughly and outlined a plan of action. First, he would go into the community and seek out some of the potential leaders and discuss the idea of a neighborhood corporation. This procedure would involve explaining the purpose of such a corporation, its organization, the writing of by-laws, and the election of a board of directors (only one-third required to be poor) and officers. We had had previous experience with a similar group at Vinson Street in Williamson, which had organized and drawn up a set of by-laws and received a state charter.

Since late July, Cletis had been spending two days a week in Dingess, talking with as many people as possible about the corporation, and he had received an enthusiastic response. Some, however, still feared that Della would hand-pick the persons she wanted elected. Certainly that was a distinct possibility. We were hoping that, if she made a fight to keep Maxine as chairman, we could possibly split some people away from her if enough of them would stand up.

During the last week in October, Cletis had come into my office and informed me that he was going to attempt an organizational meeting of the corporation on Friday evening, just two days away. "Are there any last minute instructions or suggestions you want to make?" he asked.

"Do you feel, Cletis, that you have enough people who are sold on the idea?" I asked.

"Yeah, if we aren't able to do it now, then we may as well write Dingess off because I don't know anything else we can do." He was standing directly in front of my desk and appeared to be eager to give the plan a try.

"The only thing I can tell you, Cletis, is go ahead and raise a little hell, but don't raise more than you can handle."

He looked at me and smiled. He knew what I meant. As he was leaving, he said, "I will let you know how it turns out."

When Cletis arrived for the meeting at the Dingess grade school, he was surprised to see more than a hundred cars parked on the playground and around the building. People were standing all around, a few in small groups, some talking about the meeting and others just talking about the weather. At 7:00 P.M., everyone went inside the school lunchroom for the meeting. Maxine and Della moved to the front of the room and sat down at a table facing the crowd. Della's sons Hugh and Wink stood at the left, leaning against the wall, with their eyes cast upon Cletis as he moved to the front to take his place beside Maxine.

Maxine rose to her feet amidst all the chatter of the crowd and called the meeting to order. "If you people will quieten down," she said, "we will start the meeting. I understand we have a visitor here from the office." The people in Dingess always referred to everyone who worked for the EOC as being "from the office." "I don't know what he has called this meeting for, so I figure the best thing is to let him tell you about it. The only thing I can add is there has been a poverty program here in this county for several months, and I can't see a thing they have done for us."

It was certainly true that not much had been accomplished in Dingess. There had never been any organization of the poor that had attempted to identify and solve their own problems.

Complete silence greeted Cletis when he rose to his feet. Wink sat down. Somewhat nervous, Cletis arrived at the point quickly and explained that he was there to discuss the possibility of establishing a neighborhood corporation made up of low income people. "I have brought with me a copy of the by-laws that the people of Vinson Street drew up for their organization, and I think I should read them so you could have some understanding as to what it is all about."

Moving from the wall toward the center of the room, Della's son Hugh shouted, "Let me tell you something right now, Mr. Blackburn. What you have in your hand is a set of nigger by-laws drawed up by them niggers on Vinson Street. Now we are white people down here, and we ain't going to be ruled by a set of nigger laws."

The crowd became excited. Some shouted disappointment at Hugh's statement; others agreed with him. His brother Wink, now back on his feet, walked up behind Cletis as if to strike him.

54

Hol Hannah, a retired coal miner in his early fifties, asked for Cletis to be heard. "I say to you people, we ought to hear this man out. We have come here to listen to him, and I think we ought to hear what he has to say."

"You are right, Hol. We've listened to the Wellmans long enough. It's time we started listening to someone else for a change," said Lorraine Parsley. Her voice trembled as she attempted to support Hannah's statement.

But, as Cletis appeared to be gaining some support from the group, Hugh interrupted again: "We are not going to have a meeting here tonight."

Maxine rose to her feet. "This meeting is adjourned."

Hugh Wellman rushed to the corner of the room and switched the lights off. "Everybody go home. This meeting is over!" he shouted.

Many of the group were spellbound, some plainly disgusted with the behavior of the Wellmans. People started moving slowly from the room. A small group clustered around Cletis as he left the building. Oscar Dingess, a young man with prematurely gray hair, yelled at Cletis, "Are you going to give up now, or are you coming back?"

"What do the people want?" Cletis asked.

"We want you back. We are sick and fed up with Della Wellman's outfit, and, if we don't make a stand now, we may as well give up. I believe there is enough good people down here to resist her if you are willing to give it another try."

"Yeah, let's get the people out again. It will be different next time. I have lived here all my life, and I am tired of this injustice that is coming from the Wellman family," exclaimed Uncle Jim Marcum. "But I want to tell you one thing, Cletis; don't go through the tunnel tonight. You

55

don't know them people like I do. They'll kill you down there."

Cletis listened intently but did not take the statement seriously. "I'll be back if you people want me, but I would like for some of you to call the office and talk with Mr. Perry about the situation down here, or either a carload could come to the office."

"We'll come to the office tomorrow," said Lorraine Parsley.

Most of the crowd was leaving. The Wellmans were inside, except for Hugh, who was standing at the top of the steps eying the remaining people, with a very watchful look directed toward Cletis and the fifteen or twenty people gathered around him. Shortly, Della and her son Wink came out, and they left with Hugh.

"Cletis, I still say you should not go home tonight; it's hard to tell what will happen," said Joe Grubb.

"Well, I don't think they will try anything, and I will be careful. You let me know when you want me back, and I'll be here."

Hol Hannah suggested Monday evening, and everyone agreed.

Cletis walked to his car and started home. Not all was lost, he thought. Many of the people were now more determined than they had been to organize the Dingess area. Uncle Jim Marcum and Joe Grubb had been blunt. Driving toward the tunnel, Cletis recalled the two statements and the warnings made by Marcum and Grubb, and, being alone now, he did not feel very sure of his decision. For a moment, he thought that maybe he should have gone home with one of them, but again he reassured himself that nothing would happen.

As he approached the entrance to the tunnel, Cletis could hear the water dripping from the ceiling, and he could smell the musty air. It was just like the entrance to a coal mine—the same smell and the same darkness. He knew that, if he made it through the tunnel, everything would be all right. He wished he were already through it.

When he was about two hundred feet inside the tunnel, a car, which was parked in the middle of the tunnel, turned on its lights and started toward him. He threw his car in reverse and backed out of the tunnel as fast as possible, bouncing over the chug holes. The bottom of his vehicle was taking a furious beating. Once he was outside the tunnel, another car, parked on a road that led over the tunnel —seldom used because it was impassable most of the time— turned on its lights and started down the hill toward the main road.

Almost in panic, Cletis turned his car around and drove as fast as possible back down Twelve Pole Creek toward Dingess, hoping to overtake some of his friends who had been at the ill-fated meeting. Noticing that he had outdistanced the two pursuing cars, he turned his lights off and pulled onto a side road, which was hidden from the main highway. His heart thumped as both cars sped past. Fearing that he would be discovered if he attempted to move, he remained on the side road in the dark until 3:00 A.M. Finally, at 3:15, after he had ventured through the tunnel, this time without incident, he met Chafin and two state policemen. They were searching the highway along the Laurel fishing lake, feeling that, if any violence had come to Cletis, it would have happened there.

It was close to 4:00 when Chafin called me. As I started toward the airport, without sleep, it was frightening to have to think how far some people would go to keep others from organizing to help themselves. I found myself thinking of my father's stories about the threats and violence that had accompanied the movement to unionize the coal miners in the early 1900's. It was hard to believe the events that had just happened, harder still to accept them, and I tried to push them from my mind.

6

In Morgantown, I discussed the problem of Dingess with Dom Garafalo. Dom was a short, dark-complexioned Italian, who had worked in West Virginia as a labor organizer with the AFL-CIO. Born in south Philadelphia, he became a union organizer at the age of seventeen. He had been with the OEO since its inception, first working in eastern Kentucky and finally becoming the district director for the state of West Virginia.

When I explained the near violence at the Dingess meeting and the threat and danger to Cletis, he became very excited and angry. Although there was little he could say or do, at least he understood some of the obstacles we were meeting in our efforts to organize the poor.

Early on Monday morning, a big man in faded bib overalls and an old red hunting shirt came to the EOC office in Williamson, completely out of breath. He had walked up the stairs instead of riding the elevator.

"Where's Perry?" he asked.

"He's in his office," Donna replied. "May I tell him your name?"

"Why, I am Frank Blair, and I think it's important I see Perry."

She buzzed me, and I invited Blair in.

"Damned if I ain't out of breath. Walking up them three sets of stairs is rough on a man," he declared.

When I inquired why he had not taken the elevator, he said that he didn't know how to operate it.

"Perry, now it ain't none of my business, but I read in the paper what happened to this feller Blackburn down at Dingess the other night. Now, I live on this side of the tunnel, but I know every one of them over there. I just don't want you to give in to them. And I want to tell you something else. Now, they'll kill you over there. Why, there has been seventeen constables and deputy sheriffs killed over there that I know of personally."

He pulled a red handkerchief from his back pocket, blew his nose, and then continued, "And that Della Wellman and her outfit are tied right in with Noah Floyd. Anything that goes on down there, he knows all about it. Now, son, you are young, and I am an old man. Ain't got but a few years left in this old world. You listen; I know what I am talking about. My own brother Morrie is tied in right with them. Do you know Morrie?"

Before I could answer, he explained that Morrie was the jailer and a part-time deputy sheriff. "He tells me what they are thinking, and, believe me, they want you out of the county. They are feared you are going to tear up their little playhouse," he said, leaning over to spit in the wastebasket beside my desk and using his sleeve to wipe the tobacco juice from the corner of his mouth.

He continued, "Now that Della's been in power down there so long, everybody is scared to death of her. If you

60

don't do what she says, she will have Noah cut your check off, or, if you are working on the crash program, she is liable to have you moved plum on the other end of the county. And, if you can't get to work, they'll cut you off the program."

He reached into his pocket and rattled some pieces of metal by shaking his hand, then looked at me and grinned. "I'll bet you don't even know what that means."

"I am afraid not, Mr. Blair."

He pulled from his pocket a handful of 30-30 automatic rifle shells. "You see, the people in Dingess have a warning. You know how an old rattlesnake will sing and warn you before he strikes? Well, if you ever hear that noise, you'll know someone is warning you that they are going to get you. You didn't know that, did you?" He smiled again.

"No, sir," I replied, "but I'm glad you told me."

He looked me over carefully. "You are big enough," he said. "Do you have a gun?"

"No, sir, I don't."

"Then don't go back in there without one. You do plan to go back to Dingess and help them people out, don't you?"

"Yes, we have talked with several people in Dingess, and they want us to come back," I said. "We plan to hold a meeting in two days."

He looked at me very seriously. "Now, Perry, you are going to hear a lot of metal rattling before everything is settled. But, if you will stop and get me, I'll go with you to Dingess. And, if we hear any rattling, I'll rattle back. I never go in there unless I take my gun."

He talked several more minutes, telling me all he knew about Dingess. When he was through, I felt that I knew the area and its people somewhat better. But I was also concerned for my own safety and for the safety of the staff. Before he left, I promised to pick him up on Wednesday, and he described his house and its proximity to the tunnel.

Later in the afternoon, I received calls from reporters with the Associated Press and the *Huntington Herald Dispatch*. They had read the news story of the Dingess incident in the *Williamson Daily News*. Both wanted to know whether we planned to go back into Dingess and whether they could be present at the next meeting. I explained that we would be glad to have them go along if they were willing to take the risk. They were to meet me in Williamson on Wednesday afternoon.

During the next two days, more than twenty people from Dingess came into Williamson to encourage us to organize the area and to urge us not to back away. Each told of the violence that from time to time had erupted between families. They told of unsolved murders, of bushwhacking, and of shoot-outs between political enemies. As each gave his own rendition of a particular murder, it varied a little from the others. But, regardless of the facts behind the murders, one fact was clear in my mind—they did take place. In talking with the people from Dingess, I voiced my concern about traveling through the tunnel. I felt that this would be the most likely place to be shot if someone planned any violence. Each time, the people assured me they would protect us if we went.

Larry and I spent several hours discussing the problem with the other staff members, and we all came to the same conclusion: We had to go into Dingess, and we had to organize the community to free it from the control of Della Wellman and Noah Floyd. If we failed, then community organization would fail in Mingo County. The politicians would use the same tactics in the rest of the county to take over the groups that had been organized. It was a life-and-death struggle for community action.

On Wednesday afternoon, the newspaper reporters, Jim Renneisen of the Associated Press and Dave Peyton of the *Huntington Herald Dispatch,* came down from Huntington. We felt that their presence would be advantageous to our efforts, for this would be an opportunity to expose the resistance to community action on a state-wide basis. Not only would it be healthy for Mingo, but for the rest of West Virginia as well. Every county in the state had its Noah Floyds and Della Wellmans.

We decided to leave for Dingess at 5:00 P.M. The meeting was set for 7:00 P.M. Corporal Berkley of the local state police detachment had called earlier and said that he had dispatched two patrol cars to the area and that they would escort us through the tunnel. This information offered some relief, but we knew that, if violence occurred, two policemen could not quell it. I rode in a car with Joe Smith, an OEO field analyst who had come in from Washington as an observer. Larry and two other staff members were also in the car. No one was talking about Dingess or saying what he anticipated would happen at the meeting.

As we approached the tunnel, dusk had already turned into darkness. As we turned the final curve before the tunnel, the headlights of our car revealed several parked automobiles and people milling about up and down the highway. It turned out to be a very pleasant surprise. Twenty-eight carloads of Dingess residents had come through the tunnel to provide an escort. We stopped our car at the end of the line. I got out, quite nervous, and walked through the crowd.

"Huey Perry, come over here," a loud voice shouted

through the darkness. I could see puffs of cigarettes flickering from bright to dim all up and down the road.

"I would like for you to know we ain't going to back down," said Hol Hannah, as I walked toward where he was huddled with several others from the area.

"No, sir, we ain't going to back down," said Oscar Dingess.

I indicated that we were with them and that we were determined to organize the community. I asked Hol what Della would do that night.

He replied, "Your guess is as good as mine. But, let me tell you, everybody here has a gun, and they know how to use it." He pulled his coat back and showed me the revolver he had placed in his belt.

Jim Renneisen of the Associated Press was standing beside me and listening to the conversation. When we started back to our car, he wanted to know whether I thought there would be violence.

"Jim, if you want to know the truth, I am scared to death."

I felt secure as far as getting through the tunnel safely was concerned, but I fully realized that a violent duel between the two factions could rage at the meeting in the grade school.

Hol Hannah rode in our car. He informed me that Leslie Wellman, a Freewill Baptist minister, was in the group. He said that Wellman was deeply concerned over the hostilities that had occurred at the previous meeting and felt that it was his duty as a minister to help the poor. It was reassuring to know that fundamentalist religion was not going to be a force to deal with in Dingess as it had been in other parts of the county.

As we made the final turn to a dirt road leading to the

school, I asked Hol whether he thought Della would have the school door open. Because she was the janitor, she had the only keys, and she was obligated by state law to open the building for any public meeting.

He replied, "I don't know. Someone said she had to go to Huntington."

When we arrived, several people had already parked their cars and were standing around in front of the school. Della's crowd was nowhere in sight—only the people who had met us on the other end of the tunnel, and there were about 150 of them.

Reverend Wellman had been one of the first to arrive, along with Oscar Dingess, and they had examined the door. Oscar yelled, "It's locked."

Someone yelled from the corner of the schoolyard, "Break the goddamned thing down! They're not going to lock us out."

"Yeah, break it down!"

By this time, the entire crowd had gathered in front of the school. The only light came from a small 100-watt bulb that hung directly over the door. Now and then, I could make out a face as some of the men scurried to the door.

"Let's tear it down!"

Even Reverend Wellman had become angered by the locked door. He yelled, "Get me a hammer, and I'll break the lock. This is a public building, and we intend to use it."

Oscar Dingess yelled out, "Wait a minute; I've got one in my car."

Several of the men were striking on the door. Renneissen walked over to where I was standing and asked, "Are you going to let them tear it down?"

Suddenly I realized that I, too, had been carried by the

crowd's actions and had not taken time to think about the repercussions that could come from breaking into a public building. Without answering Renneissen, I walked up to the door and asked Reverend Wellman whether he thought it was a good idea to break in the door. I suggested it might be a strategy of Della Wellman's to set up such an incident in order to gain public support in her behalf.

He answered, "Now, you may just have a point there. Since she lives over there on the hill, why don't we drive over there and see if she really went to Huntington. If not, we'll make her let us have her key."

Although I was hesitant about trespassing on her private property, I agreed to go along. The Reverend Wellman then asked for the attention of the crowd and explained what we were going to do.

The crowd quieted down and awaited our return. But the trip was unsuccessful, for there was no one at Della's home. At least no one answered the door, and the lights were turned off.

Ersel Prince, the operator of a small sawmill, suggested that the group go to his house for the meeting. He had a huge basement that would hold everyone. Reluctantly, the group decided to move the meeting. By now, I felt much better about being able to organize Dingess. Because the Wellmans did not show at the school, I assumed they were backing away, perhaps because so many people were determined to organize the community.

Once the crowd had reassembled in the Prince basement, Reverend Wellman asked for silence. "Friends, I think we should open this meeting with a prayer, and, since there are more preachers here than myself, I am going to call upon Brother Marcum to lead us in prayer."

66

Marcum, a tall, lean man in his early fifties, stepped to the center and asked everyone to bow his head. "God, we thank thee for giving us the privilege to meet here tonight in Brother Prince's home. Oh, God, may you look out after all of us so that we might make this a better community, not only for our friends but for all them people that has fought us so hard. God, we ask in thy name to forgive them. Bless the poor, oh Lord, and bless the elderly, oh Lord. May we congregate here in peace and love, and may we work in harmony for the sake of the community, and for the sake of thee, oh Lord. Bless these men who have come to meet with us, oh Lord, and guide them in your ways. Amen."

"Thank you, Brother Marcum, for that wonderful prayer. And now, I'll turn this meeting over to Mr. Perry from Williamson."

During the next ten or fifteen minutes, I explained the purpose of a neighborhood corporation and described the steps citizens must take to become organized. I explained the role of the officers and the board of directors, all of whom here in Dingess would be elected from the poor. Some asked a few questions concerning the state charter, but, other than that, they were ready to conduct business.

During the next thirty minutes, the group selected a board of directors and elected officers. The new corporation was named the Harvey District Community Action Group, and Oscar Dingess was elected president. He immediately assumed his role: "Since Mr. Perry has explained that we need to get together to draw up a set of by-laws, I suppose we should meet again within the next two or three days." A woman in the back of the room suggested that the board of directors meet first to draw up by-laws and then submit them to the group for approval. This suggestion was quickly agreed upon, and it was decided that the board would meet within two days to draft the by-laws.

Near the end of the meeting, the crowd became jubilant. Someone shouted, "We're free now! At last, we cooked the 'old blue goose'!"

For the first time in years, the people of Dingess had made a decision that would affect the entire community, and Della Wellman had not been present nor had any part to play in what had happened. On the contrary, she would probably continue to oppose community action in Dingess.

Although we knew there was a tremendous amount of work yet to be done, the entire staff was pleased with the meeting. As we headed back into the tunnel, we had an escort of two state troopers—one in the front and one in the rear—and four carloads of community people, all armed with guns.

During the following weeks, the Dingess group continued to meet on a weekly basis. Sometimes there were as many as three hundred people in attendance. However, not all was quiet. The AFDCU enrollees had been ordered to stay away from the meetings, and, as a result, the group was making plans to expose the corruption that existed in the program. Reports were circulating through the county that AFDCU enrollees were working on the private property of the politicians. A report from Dingess indicated that one of the supervisors hired by the State Road Commission was working the men in his own personal timber operation, and one of Della Wellman's sons had been accused of using the men to remodel homes with aluminum siding.

The community action groups believed that the AFDCU program was a worthwhile one that could provide some income to many unemployed fathers who could not find jobs in the county. At the same time, they felt that the program should be free from county politics. Each group also wanted to participate in planning projects for its own community. In many instances, people wanted their own hollow roads repaired.

Believing that it was impossible to get the State Department of Welfare to investigate the AFDCU program in Mingo County, the Harvey District Community Action Group scheduled a public hearing in the Williamson high school auditorium. The meeting was publicized in the *Williamson Daily News.*

7

What appeared to be an endless line of cars moved slowly up Mulberry Street toward Williamson High School. The athletic field, which was used as a parking lot, had already been filled, and both sides of the street were lined with parked cars. Hundreds of people were standing around outside the school.

I arrived about 9:30 A.M., in time to discuss the agenda with Ersel Prince, whom the group had chosen to moderate the meeting. Ersel was quite nervous. We both knew that this was a critical meeting for community action—the first major public confrontation with the local political establishment.

The big question in everyone's mind was whether the local politicians would appear for the meeting. This question was soon answered. It was Uncle Jim Marcum who first noticed the caravan of cars and pointed out Noah. "Well," he said, "I guess all of our questions are answered now. Here comes Noah and all them politicians from the courthouse, and, by the looks of the cars following him, I guess he's got all the workers down there with him."

Oscar Dingess chimed in, "Yeah, there's Della and her two sons in that third car behind Noah."

As the caravan moved slowly up the hill, it was evident that the entire Democratic organization had decided to attend the meeting. Noah was the first to get out of his car. Walking across the school lawn, he was shaking hands with everyone who was facing in his direction.

The politicians had been disturbed by a full-page advertisement that had appeared in the local *Williamson Daily News* on Friday. It had accused the local politicians of using the AFDCU program to perpetuate their own machine through the use of force and intimidation of the welfare recipients.

Glancing out of the corner of my eye, I observed that Noah obviously was working himself toward our small group. He was stopping occasionally to chat with people he knew. He was followed by Steve Adkins, the sheriff; Tom Chafin, the County Court clerk; and several of the clerk-typists who worked in the courthouse.

Stationed throughout the crowd and inside the building were several constables and deputy sheriffs. They were making no effort whatsoever to assist the people in parking their automobiles or to direct the congested traffic. Evidently, the local politicians had anticipated problems or were going to make an effort to have their renegades disrupt the entire hearing. By 9:50, practically every political figure in the county had arrived for the meeting. The entire Democratic Party executive committee was present.

Finally, Noah worked his way through the crowd to our group. He was the first to speak, extending his hand to me and then to Larry. He looked at me and said, "Perry, are you going to moderate this meeting, or who's in charge here?" He was chewing on a cigar and had his coat buttoned all the way to the top. The weather was extremely chilly.

"Mr. Ersel Prince has been selected by the community action group to moderate the meeting," I replied.

Ersel knew Noah only by name and had never met him personally. "Who is this fellow, Perry?" he asked.

I answered, "This is the man you've been hearing a lot about in this county. This is Noah Floyd. He is the state senator from Mingo and also chairman of the Democratic Party."

Noah extended his hand and said, "I'm glad to meet you, Mr. Prince. Perry tells me you're going to moderate this meeting."

Ersel, who was not always easy to understand, replied, "Yeah, I reckon I am. The group down in my part of the country decided I oughta be the man to moderate the meeting, and I guess I'll do the best I can."

Noah glanced backward, "Hey, Steve, come over here a minute. I want you to meet Ersel Prince from Dingess. He's going to moderate this meeting."

Working his way through the crowd, Steve made his way over to our group, where he shook hands with Ersel, me, and several other people who were standing around.

Noah said, "Actually, Mr. Prince, the only thing I wanted to see you about is to see if I could have time on the program. And, in fact, I would like to sit on the stage."

Ersel answered, "Well, I don't guess there's anything wrong with that. If you want to sit on the stage, I suppose you can."

Looking over at me, Noah asked, "Are you going to sit on the stage, Perry?"

"This is a meeting conducted by the people of Dingess," I said. "But, since you're going to sit on the stage, I suppose I probably should sit there, too."

"Could you and I walk over here and talk just a minute before this meeting starts?" Noah asked me. "And, Larry, I'd like to talk with you, too."

We moved away from the crowd to the far corner of the school building. I sensed that Noah was disturbed by the large size of the crowd at the meeting. Although he had summoned his entire gang, his supporters were outnumbered. It was a welcome sight to witness that the other community action groups in the county had sent representatives to the meeting in support of Harvey District.

Noah, looking directly at me, said, "Now I don't know, Perry, what has inspired you to call such a meeting, but you're gonna tear up everything here in this county with this kind of thing."

"Mr. Floyd," I said, "I'm not the man responsible for this meeting. As you obviously read in the *Williamson Daily News,* the Harvey District Community Action Group is the sponsor, and I think the advertisement stated the purpose of the meeting."

Noah countered, "Now, you don't think I'm dumb enough not to know that you're the man behind this. You're the one that's gone out all over this county and stirred the people up. You've got them to thinking that we're all a bunch of crooks. Now, you know, Perry, if it hadn't been for me, you wouldn't have had this job. I'm the very man that recommended you for it, and I don't know what you have got against me."

I assured Noah that I did not have anything personal against him. At the same time, I pointed out that I disagreed with many of his policies, especially the treatment that many poor people were receiving. I implied that he was, either directly or indirectly, responsible.

He then asked me whether there was any way whatsoever that the meeting could be called off. I explained to him that it was impossible at this late date even to think about it. By now, most of the crowd had gathered. The auditorium, including the balcony in the rear, seated approximately six hundred people. All the seats were already taken, and people were standing against the walls.

As we turned to walk into the building, Noah once again complained that I was going to tear up the Democratic Party within the county. I suggested that he should talk with Ersel Prince because he was the man who was going to moderate the meeting.

By then, it was 10:05 and Ersel had already proceeded to the stage. As we walked down the aisle, there was a considerable amount of chatter. On the stage, I took a seat to the right of Joe Spry, a member of the Harvey District Community Action Group. Floyd sat at Joe's left.

Spry greeted me and said, "How are you, Perry? There sure is one heck of a crowd out there, ain't there?"

Looking back over the crowd, I noticed that the politicians had strategically placed themselves in various positions throughout the entire auditorium.

Ersel began the meeting by asking the Reverend Roscoe Marcum to lead the group in prayer. As Reverend Marcum walked up to the stage, Ersel motioned with his hands for the crowd to rise. Marcum, a lay Freewill Baptist minister from Dingess, was in his mid-fifties and had a very loud voice.

"Oh Heavenly Father, we pray here today that you will

74

give a blessing to all those that are here to participate in this meeting. Help us to understand their problems, and guide these men in the righteous way. Give them the knowledge to make this a better county, and may we leave here today with a better understanding. We pray in thy name. Amen."

Once the crowd had settled down again, Ersel began, "My name is Ersel Prince, and I'm from Dingess, West Virginia. I suppose most of you have heard of that place one time or another."

He was looking straight ahead, with both hands holding tight to the rostrum. "Now, I'm not an educated man, nor do I claim to be an educated man. And I ain't much of a speaker. But, as I stand here before this congregation today, I am hopeful, as a result of this meeting, that we can have a better understanding about these here programs. Now, I am a taxpayer in Mingo County, and what this county needs is industry, and these people working together, not just one or two, but everybody working together to make it a better county. Now, the purpose of this meeting is to discuss the 'crash program,' and we're wanting to know why these men can't be used to work on community projects that'll benefit the community rather than just a few individuals here and there."

The crowd was silent and listening very intently. We had expected Ersel to give a brief introduction and state the purpose of the meeting, but he continued to ramble on about industry for Mingo County. Many of the people from Dingess were looking toward one another in amazement that Ersel had barely mentioned the purpose of the meeting. After thirty minutes, the crowd gave him a round of applause, and he sat down.

Although I had not intended to participate in the meeting, I felt that it had become necessary for me to assist Ersel and state briefly the purpose of the meeting. Fearing that Floyd would attempt to take over, I moved rapidly to the microphone and proceeded to state as briefly as possible, why we were meeting, repeating primarily what was in the ad in the *Williamson Daily News*. Directly behind me, Noah was talking with Ersel and insisting that he now be given the floor. Overhearing the conversation, I immediately introduced Noah. There was applause from the crowd. He rose to his feet and nodded appreciation.

He stepped to the microphone, looked at the audience, and cleared his throat. He began by saying, "Good morning!" in a loud and friendly greeting, lifting both hands in front of him.

"Let's smile now; that's what we need to do."

Speaking without notes, he continued: "I'm sorry that I haven't had the pleasure of meeting you before. I think probably I know most people in the audience today, and a good many of them I can call by first name. Now, I've been in and around Mingo County all my life. I have been your representative in the state legislature and the state Senate for some fifteen years. I was in Charleston at the very inception of the program, and it can help our people in Mingo County. If you will recall, some several years ago, people in Mingo County really were destitute. We had unemployed fathers with big families who didn't have a job, bread, or anything to eat."

The audience was attentive as he intoned, "Yes, I am also a poor man."

But several people glanced at each other and grinned. If they knew one thing, they knew that Noah Floyd was not a poor man. It was hard to conceive that he would classify himself as poor when it was a known fact that he had a very lucrative position as a salesman for a large book-publishing firm and owned one of the nicest homes in the county.

Warming to the subject, he said, "I grew up as a poor boy. I grew up just as hard as you people. However, some of us have been a little more fortunate than others in that we probably had a little more at hand to move the hay. We did more on our own. Maybe the opportunity arose that we could move better. These things happen. Abraham Lincoln was that way; he was a poor boy, but he made good. A lot of it, people, depends upon you as an individual. I would like to say—"

At this point, Floyd hesitated as if he were searching for words. He was getting muddled. "There has been inferences here that the AFDCU men in Mingo County has been under bondage. Now, folks, this is not true, and I'll show you in a few minutes that it isn't."

Looking over at the section of the auditorium where most of the people from Harvey District were seated, he said, "Now this happens to come from one little particular section in Mingo County, and I'll show you that it is only from one section." He again pointed to the section of the auditorium where the men and women of Dingess were sitting.

People were not understanding what he was saying, but he continued, "Now, speaking of Harvey District, when did you get your road hard-topped from Dingess to Breeden? Who started the new improvements on the tunnel to get it passable so that we could restore it and, at the same time, make it passable?"

Several from the Harvey District group shouted out, "We did! We were the ones that went to Charleston and got the State Road Commission to work on the Dingess tunnel."

Noah ignored the heckling and proceeded: "That's been in the process even before the group talked about it. Now we have other plans over there. I don't have those plans; your county road supervisor handles that, Mr. Johnny Owens. He can show you. You go over the county and look. Look at the hollow and creek roads. There are roads that have been hard-topped and repaired that have never been done before in the history of the county."

Noah continued to make reference to the achievements of the local Democratic Party. Many people in the audience heckled and booed him.

Once again, he attempted to redirect the meeting by talking about bringing industry in: "Now you talk about bringing industry into Mingo County. How are you going to bring industry into Mingo County? The way we look at it, you are going to have to get a road from Huntington to Williamson. Because, if the people can't get in, surely you're not going to get any industry or anything else. This coming year, you will have a highway between Williamson and Huntington. They spent millions of dollars so that you people who are unemployed can drive to Huntington to work, drive to Kenova and work, and still live here. But why the road to Charleston? So that you can get up through that area and work."

Noah's reasoning was absurd. Everybody knew that it would take more than roads to bring employment to Mingo County. Besides, people were not interested in working in Charleston or Huntington. They wanted jobs in Mingo County. Both Huntington and Charleston were a hundred miles distant from the center of Mingo County. The reaction from many of the people in the audience indicated that they were astonished that Floyd would make such remarks. Many laughed, and Floyd immediately recognized that he probably had said the wrong thing.

His next attempt was to convince the poor that he was interested in their plight. This strategy might have worked a year before, but not now. Too many low income people had opened their eyes to the many injustices heaped upon them by local politicians who were interested only in perpetuating themselves in office.

Noah continued, "As I said in the beginning, I started helping the poor people in Mingo County. That's where our hearts are, too. Our County Court feel that way—the sheriff, clerks, the two members of your House here. But they can't do all you want. Neither can anyone else. LBJ isn't doing all you want. If he was, you would have your roads in Harvey District and everywhere around. And the state is limited in the amount of money that they can spend. Why? Because you and I have been working and paying income taxes to the state government and the federal government, and they have to pool all that money together and make it go so many miles that they can build."

At this point, Noah changed the subject to an advertisement that had appeared in the local paper. "I'd like to know from the people here this morning who feel that you have been coerced in any manner by the elected officials of Mingo County. I would like for you to stand. Anyone that has been coerced in Mingo County in any manner, I would like for you to stand right now. I'd just like to see who you are. I'd like to know if there is anyone."

He hesitated as he looked over the crowd.

There was a burst of chatter from the audience. Between seventy-five and a hundred people immediately rose to their feet, and most of the people in the auditorium applauded, for it took a lot of courage to stand up in front of the local political machine. Noah seemed startled that anyone, let alone so many, would have the nerve to stand up, and he was at a loss for words.

Finally, he said, "Now that's all you have. Out of this entire group, only a few."

Then, in an effort to counteract the effect of the people who said they had been coerced, he asked, "Out of this whole group that is here, how many now can stand and say that they haven't been?"

All of the elected officials, State Road bosses, and executive committee men and women stood, along with many of their relatives. As they sat back down, Noah said, "Thank you very much. I'd like to say this. Now, you talk about the welfare program. Who do you think has helped you to get your food orders? Who do you think has helped you to get on the program to start with? Hasn't your County Court, your sheriff, the county clerk, the members of the House? Anytime you've come, haven't they helped you?"

Again, there was applause (although many observers later said that this was merely Floyd's way of reminding the many welfare recipients who were present that they could possibly lose their welfare checks for stating that they had been coerced).

"Now, we have plans for your roads in Harvey District. But that, like everything else, you have people who you've always worked with that know generally what is going on. The road supervisor, his foreman over there who he works with, he has plans." He pointed toward Johnny Owens, who was sitting in the front row, along with his assistant. Owens was in his early forties, swarthy, and had a small mustache. He looked embarrassed.

"Now, we're going to do it for you, but we have an overall plan by which we operate. Now, those people in the Magnolia District, Stafford District, Lee District, or Williamson, and everywhere else, they have to leave it up to the ones in authority. You can't go in and hard-top twenty miles of dirt road that has some twenty families on it. Put all your money in a little spot like that—you just can't do it. And you have to be frank."

Noah, by this time, was incoherent, jumping from one subject to another. As he proceeded, he made a reference to an earlier statement by Ersel Prince, who had spoken of working together. Again holding both hands high, he said, "Now, he spoke of working together. Now, this is what we want, people. If you are really interested in helping yourselves, now, the thing to do is to get with your leaders in the districts in which you live, and let's all work together and get what you want."

He was telling the people that, if they would cooperate with the executive committees from each of the districts and continue to be controlled, he, too, would cooperate with them. At this, there was loud heckling from the audience, and it was almost a minute before he could continue.

"Now, the way that you're going about it, you're going against—" He began searching for words. "You're just diametrically opposed to the way that you ought to do it. If you're going to get something done, you've got to work with people. You don't work against them. You are creating animosities to start with. Now look, you are poor people. We're all poor people. There's no wealthy people in here. Now I see some people back there that I taught school with for years. Mrs. Evans, she can vouch for that. Over here—." (He pointed to an elderly woman who sat midway in the auditorium.)

"We've helped little children get their breakfast and lunch, anytime they wanted to eat, clothes—we've even given them a bath in school. Now, if that isn't for poor people, what else could you do? And, as I say, we in the legislature—and I speak for Mr. Simpkins and Mr. Varney, both—we have consistently supported programs that would help the poor people, that would help union workers, wage earners; and, if you don't believe it, look at the records. That speaks for itself. You look at the over-all construction of roads in Mingo County. There's no one, no one in the history of the county that can match that.

"We are working for you when you are sleeping, trying to help you get something that you haven't. Who got the lake up at Laurel? Some $400,000 was spent up there. All right now, you're going to have another couple hundred thousand dollars spent. The roads have been hard-topped up there twice. We're going to eventually get a contract job from Dingess to Breeden, from Dingess to Maher. But you have to fit it into the respective place.

"Now, before I quit, I would like to say this: I would like for you to see your elected officials in case you don't know them." Pointing to Steve Adkins, he continued, "I would like for you to see the sheriff of Mingo County, Steve Adkins." Noah motioned with his hands for Steve to stand, and there was brief applause. He continued the introductions: "Three members of your County Court—Harry Artis, Shorty Myers, and Ben Hamilton—County

Clerk Tom Chafin, Assessor Arnold Starr, and the two members of the House are Bob Simpkins and T. I. Varney." All stood and bowed as they received applause.

At this juncture, Noah was evidently feeling somewhat more confident than he had felt during the previous part of his talk. "Now, folks, I would like to conclude in this. If you really, if you really are interested in helping yourselves, there is only one way to do it. That's all of us working together. Now, before I quit, I'd like for a fellow to stand who I have heard reports on, and everybody else has, that the roads have been in better shape in Mingo County, snow-wise and otherwise, than has ever been in the history of Mingo County." He motioned for Johnny Owens to stand, and there was brief applause.

"Now, if you are really interested—and I have no personal malice toward anyone—I'll work with you regardless of who you are, because I am your county chairman and your state senator. I'm interested in your problems, but I'm interested in you working with us, not against us. Thank you very much."

As he sat down, there was loud applause from his cheering section. I immediately stepped to the microphone and asked whether anyone had a question he wanted to ask.

Hi Marcum, the man who had first telephoned me concerning Cletis, rose to his feet and said that he had a few. I invited him to come to the stage and speak through the microphone so that everyone could hear. Marcum walked to the stage, his hands visibly shaking.

"The first thing I have for business is with Mr. Floyd. You say we should work together. Now, how can we work together when you want us to bow down, bow down to these politicians in our community and do what they say?"

Noah immediately rose to his feet. "Mr. Marcum, I'll be happy to answer that question. As you know, in a democracy, the majority rules. That's always been the case. That's why I'm proud to be an American, because the majority rules." He proceeded to tell Marcum that the committeemen and committeewomen in his district were elected by the people and that, as a result of their being elected by the people, everyone should work with them regardless of what they believed. Then he sat down.

Pulling a paper from his back pocket, Hi Marcum said, "I have a question or two I would now like to ask in reference to the AFDCU program. I would like to know who authorized the State Road supervisors in Harvey District to waste $5,000 a day in taxpayers' money."

Most people in the audience knew that Marcum was making reference to the many AFDCU enrollees in Harvey District who were not required to work. The enrollees were assigned to the State Road Commission, and the foreman of the AFDCU men in Harvey District was the son of Della Wellman. The people who participated in community action and belonged to the Harvey District group contended that the only project that the Wellman son was interested in was getting the AFDCU enrollees to vote for the Democratic ticket. As long as they voted for the machine ticket, they were not obligated to work. However, if an enrollee deviated and it became known that he had voted against the machine, he was likely to be removed from the program or transferred to a remote section of the county.

Marcum continued by stating that he had talked with several AFDCU men in the district and that some had not worked for thirty days. He said that he had asked one of the men how he got by without working, and the man replied, "You have to know how to vote."

There was loud clapping. Noah rose to his feet and asked whether Marcum would like him to answer that. Marcum said, "Yes," and stepped aside.

Noah moved to the microphone. "I expect I could go out here and have hearsay from most everyone. As to those people who have been told that, if they would have confronted the county road supervisor, Mr. Owens, or any of the elected officials, I am certain this thing would have been corrected."

A roar of laughter interrupted Floyd, but he continued, "However, in a program as large as this, you can get all the insinuations and innuendos that you want from any source of any kind, so I would suggest that those people that have these complaints bring them to your county road supervisor, Mr. Owens, and I know Mr. Owens very well, and he certainly doesn't condone them."

Again there was laughter, mixed with scattered applause.

Hi Marcum went on to give a full account of how an AFDCU worker had reported to him that he was forced to pay $10 a month to the road supervisors and had also informed him that the entire crew was paying the supervisor.

Johnny Owens, the county supervisor, jumped to his feet and ran to the stage. He took the microphone from Marcum and said, "I'm Johnny Owens. I think it is about time for me to answer a couple of these questions." He insisted that Marcum name names.

"I have the names," Marcum replied, "but I do not intend to release them in a public meeting. However, I will make them public to the press."

Owens countered, "Have you got something to hide?"

"The only thing that I have told you here is exactly what the man told me himself."

Noah, who was sitting directly behind Johnny Owens, saw that the meeting was getting somewhat out of order and attempted to coach Johnny. "Johnny, why don't you just make a statement?" he asked in a very low voice.

Owens responded to Noah's suggestion: "I didn't intend to get up here, but it looks like I've been forced to." Turning away from the audience and looking toward Marcum, Owens asked, "Mr. Marcum, you used to be a Democrat, didn't you?"

"Yeah, and I still am," Marcum replied immediately, and he received loud laughter and applause.

Owens attempted once more to address the audience: "I never collected a dime—" He got no farther with his statement. The audience jeered and hooted so vehemently that he could not speak.

Finally, the county road supervisor began yelling to the many individual people who were asking him questions from the audience. Floyd jumped to his feet, walked to the microphone, and attempted to quiet everybody.

"I'd like to make this statement, please. If you're all going to talk, none of you will have a chance. I would like to make this statement, and I am sure Mr. Owens will verify it. If he ever stoops so low to ask an AFDCU person for ten dollars for a political campaign, then he doesn't need to be the road supervisor to begin with."

More applause. Noah sat back down, and Owens once again launched into an effort to explain his position to the crowd. Talking slowly and deliberately in a heavily accented mountain voice, he said, "I have never asked an AFDCU person for one dime, and there's not a one of them that can say that I have and tell the truth. And I don't intend to ever ask them."

Feeling somewhat more confident when the audience did not heckle him the second time, he changed the subject from the AFDCU payoffs and made reference to the advertisement in the *Williamson Daily News*. He asked if Joe Spry was in the house. Joe, who was sitting directly behind him, immediately replied, "Right here I am!" He bounded to his feet, and rushed to the side of Owens.

Owens said, "I believe you're the gentleman that wanted me to take an inloader and fill in around your bridge. Is that right?"

Before Johnny Owens finished his statement, Spry countered, "You didn't do it."

Owens replied, "That's right. I couldn't do it, because it was on private property, and we don't work our equipment on private property." The politicians who were supporting Owens applauded vigorously.

At this point, Spry became very angry and shouted so that the entire audience could hear him without the assistance of the microphone. "You know what you done, Johnny Owens, you went over there and scraped the East Fork of Twelve Pole Road and scraped up dirt in front of my place, and, when it would come a rain, the water had no place to go. And furthermore, we come to your office and asked you to attend our meetings, and they said you was nowhere around. Was you hiding?"

In his search for the proper answer, Owens was always saying the wrong thing as far as the Harvey District community action group was concerned, and they continued to laugh and jeer at him each time he attempted to speak.

Looking again toward Joe Spry and insinuating that it was Spry who had accused Willard Mullins, a supervisor, of using AFDCU enrollees in the private operation of a timber company, he barely got the name out before Spry interrupted, "Bring Willard Mullins to the front if he's here."

Almost a year earlier, charges had been made against Willard Mullins, stating that he had used the men illegally. However, nothing ever came of them. I had been told by many people from the Dingess area that Mullins was continuing the operation. Observing that Owens was making no effort to get Mullins to come to the stage, I interrupted and asked that Mullins please come forward if he was in the audience. There was no response, and I turned the microphone back to Owens.

He said, "I think the same charges were made a year and a half ago, and I took Mr. Mullins personally down to the district engineer's office, and I told the district engineer in front of Mr. Mullins that, if he was guilty, I wanted him fired and, if he wasn't, I wanted him cleared. And they never did prove anything on Mr. Mullins. Then the same charges were brought back a few days ago. Now, Mr. Mullins, as I understand, has seven men on the East Fork of Twelve Pole under his jurisdiction. Is that right, Mr. Mullins?"

This time Mullins rose at the back of the crowd and replied, "Yes, that is true, and I have the men here with me today, all except one. And they will all stand and say that they have never worked for me on a private timber job." Six men stood, and there was applause from the politicians.

Martha Messer, a mother from Dingess, stood and

88

shouted from the audience, "Yes, they've gotta stand up. If they don't, they know they'll be fired or transferred to some other section of the county by Monday morning."

"Now you have been accused of staying home and not putting in your time," Owens addressed the men. "I want to know whether that is true or false."

The men replied that it was false.

Next, Virgil Marcum, a young coal miner, rose to his feet in the audience and yelled, "Bring Willard Mullins up to the front. I want to ask him two or three questions." Virgil was already on his way to the rostrum.

Mullins agreed to step forward, and both men walked to the platform. When they arrived on the stage, Virgil asked Mullins, "How many men timbered for you down there a year ago and still do?"

"I don't think that's any of your business."

"Well, just wait a minute. I'm going to tell it on you." He proceeded: "There's Archie Vance and Gibb Paines."

Mullins interrupted, "Well, they're both back there, why don't you ask them?"

Marcum countered, "They're not gonna tell it on you, and you know why? Because they both live in your house. In fact, there's four of them that lives in your house, and you know damn well you've been posting. You're posting now, and you're a damn liar if you say you ain't."

Both men were so angry that it appeared the hearing might be disrupted. Several people were now arguing back and forth, and it was difficult to understand what anyone was saying. The sheriff and several of his deputies ran to the stage to calm the group. However, this action did not frighten Marcum, who continued to accuse Willard Mullins of using AFDCU enrollees to make mining timbers,

89

("posts," he called them), which were used to support mine roofs.

I was still sitting in a chair behind the microphone. So was Noah Floyd. He looked at me and said, "You'd better try to do something, for there's gonna be trouble."

When I made no effort to quell the argument, Noah became impatient and stepped to the microphone. "Now, folks, let's calm down. This is no way to settle anything. If you're gonna settle this, then we're gonna have to be quiet so we can hear each other talk. Would everybody please go back to their seat?"

After a few minutes, the crowd settled down. Willard Mullins remained on the stage, but, before he could proceed, in an effort to clear his name, his mother advanced to the platform and asked to speak.

"I'm Mr. Mullins's mother," she said, "and I live over there, and I want this crowd to know that he does let them live in his houses. Now every one of them owes him eight hundred, twelve hundred, fourteen hundred, sixteen hundred dollars in his store. Now, if these men see fit to work after they've got their hours finished, I see no wrong in that."

There was applause for Mrs. Mullins, who rushed back to her seat in the audience.

The meeting had been going on for more than an hour, and this was still part of the first episode with the politicians. I stepped to the microphone and asked whether anyone else in the house had a statement to make regarding the misuse of the AFDCU program. Lawrence Smith, who was employed as a carpenter by the Mingo County Economic Opportunity Commission, held his hand up and said that he would like to make a statement. Before working with the antipoverty agency, Smith had been an AFDCU enrollee in Magnolia District. A small, wiry man whose face showed many age lines, probably from the outside work that he had done all his life, he was known to practically everyone in the county as "Chicken" Smith.

There was quiet in the auditorium as Chicken walked to the microphone. He said, "I would like to tell this audience here of one little job that I pulled when I was on the AFDCU program. I was requested by my supervisor to build a block house and wall for Mr. Roscoe Artis on private property." There was a sustained roar from the audience, for Roscoe Artis was the father of the sheriff, Harry Artis, and this was the first evidence submitted at the hearing to indicate that elected officials were using AFDCU enrollees on private property.

Harry, sitting near the front of the room, held his head down as Chicken Smith proceeded to give the details of the work that he had performed and concluded by saying that that was the only job he had done. As he sat down, the people who supported community action gave him a standing ovation. There was silence from the opposition. Noah did not offer comment or rebuttal, nor did the sheriff.

Next, Claude Dillon, a former AFDCU enrollee, was called to the platform. There was total silence in the room. It had been rumored throughout the county that he had built a stone wall and a barbecue pit for Floyd. If this was true, it was obvious that his testimony was going to be the climactic part of the hearing. Claude was a very articulate man in his middle fifties. He had been a carpenter and stonemason and had always been able to earn a fairly decent wage, until the coal recession hit the county. He had been working for the antipoverty agency as a carpenter during the past year.

As Dillon walked to the platform, Noah sat rigidly in his

chair. He did not change expression but appeared only to be annoyed by the entire meeting. Dillon began by stating that he had worked on private property, but he did not mention any names.

Before he could proceed, Noah jumped from his chair and asked for the microphone. "Mr. Dillon—that is your name, isn't it? Claude? I don't want you to think that we would put you in a corner, because this is a democracy, and we don't operate that way. I would like to make one point clear. I've heard rumors going around that probably Claude did some private work for me at one time on private property. Now, you know I'm as frank and above-board as I can possibly be, and, if I felt that I've ever done anything wrong, I wouldn't be afraid to tell the whole world. Now, here's the case in point."

Floyd was extremely nervous and clearly felt that he must seize the initiative and explain the work that Claude had done for him before Claude had a chance to. He proceeded, "I didn't even know that Claude was on AFDCU. I give him a contract to build a little old barcebue pit out in my back yard. I furnished the rock, and he did the labor."

Laughter swept the auditorium. Noah's face tightened.

After the interruption, he continued, "Now, here's the case: Now, he did the little job for me, and I paid him. And I agree with the words that the lady said back there a few minutes ago. I believe that you people that are on AFDCU oughta be allowed to make a little money."

Hardly anyone would disagree with the statement that Noah made. However, Floyd was very much aware of the fact that the local welfare department would not allow AFDCU enrollees to earn additional money.

"I've been out to Claude's house," Noah said, and he repeated himself: "I've been out to Claude's house. And, if I could help Claude in any manner, I would do it. And, if I could give him a few extra dollars, I would do it. And I think anyone else would."

Apparently feeling that this would end the discussion, he sat down.

Claude, however, did not allow the issue to rest. Looking out over the audience, he said, "Since Mr. Floyd has named the time and the place that the work was performed, I feel that I am now out of a corner and can talk more freely about the entire matter. Mr. Floyd stated that he was not aware that I was on the AFDCU program. Now, it is a matter of record of the time that I worked while on the AFDCU program and where I worked, and Mr. Floyd should be aware of this, too. In fact, it was he who said earlier that we must see them before we are assigned to the AFDCU. Therefore, I am sure that Mr. Floyd was well aware that I was on the AFDCU program when he had me do work on his private property. While on the AFDCU, I did build a stone wall at his residence and a barbecue pit, and the only pay that we received was a little money for gasoline, since we had to drive an additional forty miles per day to get to the job. Furthermore, the stone that was used on AFDCU time was cut by AFDCU labor at Laurel Lake and hauled to Mr. Floyd's residence by AFDCU workers on AFDCU time."

There was tremendous applause throughout the auditorium, and, for a moment, everyone was anticipating Noah's next move. Floyd reluctantly stepped to the microphone.

"Now, folks," he said, "I don't think this needs an explanation. If I hire a man to do a job, I am only interested in getting the job done. The only thing I know, I paid the man. Now, if this is what's bothering the people, let me make it plain. I don't have any way of knowing who's on welfare or who's on AFDCU. I don't want to know. I think it should be an individual's right of privacy not to be known if he's on welfare. And I don't want to look down and say, 'He's on AFDCU' or 'He's on welfare.' That is the individual's own personal business."

At this point, Dillon interrupted. "Mr. Floyd, how did you know I was a stone man and I was the man you wanted to do the job?"

Noah stuttered and did not give an immediate answer. "Frankly, I couldn't answer that. It was brought to my attention by someone that you could lay a little stone. The job's out there for any of you to see. It's not a master job by any stretch of the imagination, and I think that any of you boys on AFDCU probably could build a little barbecue pit like that.

"But, frankly, I think these things are immaterial. You are creating a very bad image outside the county in the state of West Virginia and outside the state. This is certainly no way to do it. Now, if you're really interested in helping yourself, go back to your districts and meet with your leaders, whoever they be, and get right in with us and say, 'Boys, we want to work with you. We want to get some programs that'll help Mingo County. We really want to help the people of Mingo County.' But, apparently, what you're trying to do is embarrass someone. You're not going to accomplish anything this way. If you really want to do it, and you want to do a good job, I believe right in the beginning that Mr. Prince made the statement 'We need unity.' Now that's what you need—unity. You'll never get anything accomplished in the manner that you're going about it now.

"You know, in the beginning, there was no EOC in Mingo County. Do you know who's responsible for it? Your County Court. Now, if it hadn't been for your County Court, you would have never had any EOC program. Now, we were interested from the beginning, and here's what they told the Board of Directors at their first meeting. They said, 'Now, boys, we want you to take this program, divorce it in any manner from politics, but run it for the good of the people in Mingo County.' Now, fellers, the first thing we knew, they were way out in left field. Now, maybe that's the way of getting things done—by revolting and demonstrating—but I just can't see it. What we need is unity, working together, and you're not going to get it in the manner that you're going about it here today."

With that, Noah Floyd sat down.

The meeting continued for most of the day, with both sides making charges and countercharges. The next morning, the *Charleston Gazette* carried a front-page story with Noah's picture, proclaiming that he had used federally paid workers to construct a stone wall and barbecue pit on his lawn.

Some weeks later, when a member of the state legislature, Russell Davison, who had attended the public hearing, asked the House of Delegates to investigate the AFDCU program in Mingo, he was shouted down. Mingo's two delegates, Robert Simpkins and T. I. Varney, objected heatedly.

Simpkins said, "The complaints are based on the wishes of certain groups of people who desire Democratic leaders to step aside and let others take over. I feel that these people from my county contacted somebody from outside the county who does not understand our problems. In Harvey District, there are different groups, and apparently some are fighting others, and it's a matter of different groups' having different opinions about local problems. Apparently, some people working in the EOC in Mingo are in conflict with some people in the county. I don't believe such matters as this should be used in the House of Delegates to make a political picture or for any person to obtain publicity."

Besides defeating Davison's motion by a four-to-one majority, the House also voted to prohibit Davison's remarks from being printed in the House journal.

As a result of the public hearing in Williamson, the breach between the community action program and the local political machine deepened markedly.

Additional space for the EOC offices in the new courthouse was denied, whereupon it became necessary to move the antipoverty agency to Cinderella Hollow, about four miles north of Williamson. The Sycamore Coal Company had abandoned the hollow some fifteen years before, when the coal slump hit West Virginia, leaving behind an old red brick company store and office building that the EOC renovated for an office.

In the new office, directly over the door, hung an old West Virginia workmen's compensation certificate that had been issued to the Sycamore Coal Company in 1913. Perhaps because it was hanging only a foot from the twelve-foot ceiling, no one had taken the trouble to remove it. What a contrast it was to the poster on its left, sent to the office by the OEO, which seemed indicative of the burgeoning spirit of Mingo County. In bold red letters, it said, "Speak out."

8

By the end of 1966, several of the community groups had become involved with individual community projects.

The Harvey District group, after being refused permission by the Board of Education to use a school building for its meetings, constructed its own community center. It was a total community effort. A local resident donated the land, and a local bank financed the building materials. The EOC supplemented the voluntary manpower by assigning two carpenters from its home improvement program. Besides having a meeting place, the community now had a recreational center and a Head Start center. The community building rapidly became the center for all community activities.

The community of Big Branch developed a twenty-acre recreational park on top of Newsome Ridge. After the land had been cleared by volunteers from the community and Neighborhood Youth Corps enrollees supplied by the EOC, log cabins were built, picnic tables were set up, a well was drilled, and stone barbecue pits were constructed.

Other community groups developed smaller parks and

playgrounds. The community of Cinderella renovated a swimming pool that had been abandoned by the Sycamore Coal Company when the firm closed its mine. Holes were repaired, and a filtering system, which had been purchased on credit, was installed; then a bright blue coat of paint was applied. Members of the community group paid $3 a year for a family season ticket, while people from outside the community had to pay 25 cents a day. The money was used to pay for the filter and for a liability insurance policy.

Several communities established small libraries with books donated by the Council of the Southern Mountains.

The most innovative self-help project was one developed by the Gilbert Creek Community Action Group. Early in 1966, the prices of groceries all across the United States increased. The increase not only caused Midwestern house-wives to protest; it also caused the poor of Gilbert Creek to take action. I was present at a community meeting when the idea for a community-owned store that would sell at only 10 per cent above wholesale cost was presented to the group. The idea was similar to the buying club concept whereby a group of families within a community band to-gether to do their shopping collectively from a wholesaler, thus eliminating the cost of the retail merchant.

Ray Thompson, chairman of the Gilbert Creek group, had just called the meeting to order when Joyce Cline be-gan complaining about the price of food: "Why, Mr. Perry, I don't hardly see how me and my family are going to make it. There are seven of us in the family, and I only get $87 a month in food stamps, and, the way groceries cost today, we just about starve the last week of the month." Roy Ellis, a father of thirteen, agreed with Mrs. Cline.

Roy, whose vision had been impaired to the extent that he could not seek employment, was only thirty-eight years old. He had worked as a motorman for the Old War Eagle Coal Company until it closed in the early 1950's.

Roy said, "I have to pay $70 for $125 in stamps, and I only get $165 per month from the AFDCU program." Directing his statement to me, as was usual when I attended community meetings, he continued, "The other thing, Mr. Perry, I've noticed that the grocery stores in Gilbert always raise their prices at the beginning of the month, when we receive our stamps, and, at the end of the month, they always run a sale when we don't have anything to buy with. It seems to me that there ought to be something that we can do about that."

Thompson, the chairman, added to Roy's statement. "Yeah, that's the way they screw us poor people."

The discussion went on for almost an hour, with member after member telling of the hardships he faced in trying to keep enough food on the table. Occasionally, someone would complain about a doctor's bill or ask me if I could get the EOC carpentry crew to repair a roof or to build a room for some overcrowded family. But, ultimately, the discussion would come back to the price of groceries, with people complaining that they did not receive enough food stamps.

West Virginia had been the first state to introduce the food stamp plan conceived by the Kennedy Administration. In fact, McDowell County, Mingo's neighbor, was the first to implement the program. The recipient paid for the stamps according to the number in his family. For example, a family of seven paid $40 in order to receive $80 in stamps. In many ways, the program was inadequate, but it was a step better than the old commodity line it had supplanted, whereby a poor family stood in line with a box sometimes for two hours to receive only seven or eight items such as cheese, flour, beans, corn meal, powdered milk, and butter. At least, the food stamp coupon could be taken to a grocery store and the recipient could buy any type of foodstuff he desired.

During the meeting, I told the group about a buying club that had been successfully established by a group of low income blacks in Baltimore. There was much interest, and many questions came up that I could not answer, such as "We are all food stamp recipients; how could we pay for the groceries if we bought them from a wholesaler?" "What about the sales tax?" "Would we need a store license?"

I confessed that I did not know all the answers but said that I would make an inquiry as soon as possible. In the meantime, I suggested that, before the next meeting, to be held in two weeks, everybody be thinking about some type of program that could be implemented to eliminate hunger.

As I drove home that night, the statements of the Gilbert Creek poor echoed in my mind. There was no doubt that the merchants were exploiting them just as Roy had explained. I had heard of merchants' giving recipients $10 to $15 for a twenty-dollar book of food stamps. This procedure was prevalent throughout the county, particularly in the more isolated rural sections. The poor would unquestionably be better off receiving cash rather than stamps. Under the system we had, the poor had to pay a certain percentage for the food stamps and had hardly any cash left to buy clothing, to pay medical bills, to buy their children's lunches at school, or to buy household essentials such as soap and detergents, toilet paper, toothpaste, and hundreds of other items that Middle America demanded as a matter of course. I knew that in Mingo County alone three thousand families survived on less than $3,000 a year and that another thousand had less than $1,000 annual income.

The following morning, I assigned two of the staff members the tasks of researching the prices in the grocery stores of Gilbert and talking with other people in the community in an effort to document the complaints of the Gilbert Creek group. I also began researching the questions that had been raised about buying clubs.

At the next meeting, I was able to answer the questions about buying clubs, but I delayed releasing information concerning the grocery prices until the month had passed. I also discussed the idea of a cooperatively owned store, which sparked a number of questions. I explained that the co-op idea had originated hundreds of years ago in Europe and had been used successfully in the United States through the years and cited several examples of large-scale cooperatives that had been furnishing low cost products for decades.

The concept was certainly a new one for the Gilbert Creek group, but it was easy to tell from the reaction that it sparked enthusiasm.

"How much would a share cost in a grocery co-op, if this is what we decide to do?" Ray Thompson asked.

"That would depend upon a decision being made by the co-op membership. In fact, you could charge from one dollar up, I suppose."

"If I had ten shares and Elvie Ritchie had one, would I have ten votes to her one?"

"No, in a co-op each shareholder has one vote."

After thirty minutes' worth of such discussion, Roy Ellis rose to his feet and said, "I believe we all understand what Perry is talking about. Now, it seems to me that this here thing would work just as well with us poor folks here on the creek as it would in the state of Washington, with those electric co-ops, and I think we ought to organize and try it."

Seventy-year-old Floyd Lane added, "Yeah, I think we've talked about it long enough. Let's raise some money and put our own store in."

His youngest daughter, Helen, reminded him that a small store building about halfway down the creek was vacant. "Why that's right," Lane exclaimed, "and I'll bet we can get it real cheap."

The enthusiasm for the project was tremendous. Within two weeks, $5,030 in shares had been sold, and the small store building had been leased for $50 per month. Ray, Roy, and other volunteers were busy painting the inside and building shelving that would convert the one-time country store into a self-service grocery, complete with grocery carts and a self-service meat case.

In the meantime, the two staff members had completed their research and had learned that the three large stores in Gilbert, all of which were independently owned, were operating with a 25 to 35 per cent retail markup. Prices also increased an over-all 5 per cent during the first week of the month, although each store had at least five lead items that were placed on sale either at cost or about 10 per cent above cost. Two of the stores had sales on several items during the last week of the month. Some of the smaller stores that were located in the outlying areas were charging a 50 per cent markup on most items.

There was a noticeable increase in the self-confidence of the poor people of Gilbert Creek as they announced the grand-opening celebration of their store on January 2, 1967. The store had already opened a couple of weeks before Christmas, but it was decided to postpone the official celebration until the holiday season was past. An application for a food stamp authorization card had been filed with the Department of Agriculture the day the store actually opened, but, after two weeks, the authorization had not been received, and the food stamp recipients were unable to trade at the store during January. We decided that it was like most things the government bureaucracy did—all wrapped up in red tape—and that we would just have to be patient.

In mid-December, the *New York Times* had sent a reporter, Marjorie Hunter, to Appalachia to do a follow-up story on the McDowell County antipoverty agency, and someone in McDowell had told her about Mingo County and had suggested she should visit us. She spent two days in the county, spending most of her time at the Gilbert Creek store and in Gilbert, interviewing merchants and shoppers.

On Sunday morning, December 18, the *New York Times* News Service across the United States ran her story on the grocery store. One businessman had told Miss Hunter, "It's all a communist plot." She also reported, "Old line politicians are upset, and other businessmen are uneasy. But Perry, Executive Director of Mingo's lively antipoverty program, has another name for what is happening. He calls it 'poor power.' "

A score of reporters and TV newsmen followed Marjorie Hunter to Gilbert Creek. Day after day, Roy and Ray spent hours with them, going over the story of the inception of the idea of the store. For the second time, the Mingo anti-poverty program received a five-minute coverage on the Walter Cronkite news program. The Gilbert Creek co-op was the most publicized poverty project in the nation, even before the official dedication had taken place. At the same time, it was rapidly becoming the most controversial project in the United States, as well as in Mingo County.

Marjorie Hunter had been correct when she described the businessmen and politicians as being upset. Everett Rutledge, a grocery store owner in Gilbert, declared to a reporter, "There is no question it is a communist plot. I plan to write Senator Byrd and Congressman Kee and see what is going on with this poverty program in Mingo County. I thought this program was here to help the poor and not to drive us businessmen out of business. I am a taxpayer, and I intend to get to the bottom of this somehow."

Roy Ellis was chased out of two stores in Gilbert and told that he was not welcome. Other members of the group received the same type of treatment. Yet, all of these incidents did not dampen their spirits, and plans were continuing for the January 2 dedication. The group invited Dom Garafalo to be the guest speaker, and the dedication was set for 2:00 P.M.

Speaking from a truck bed to more than three hundred people, Garafalo explained that no federal money had been used to put the store in operation. He told the group, "There is nothing communistic or un-American in a co-operative!" He was interrupted by applause. "Did the merchants complain when the big coal companies opened their company stores here in the coal fields, issuing scrip that could only be spent in their own stores? Did we hear the cry of communism then?" Again he was interrupted by applause.

He concluded by reassuring the merchants of Gilbert and Mingo County that no federal funds were used in the store. I had persuaded Dom to elaborate on this point because the EOC had already been investigated twice on charges of political activity for mobilizing the poor, and I felt that continuing investigations would eventually create a credibility gap between the agency and those poor people who had not yet become involved in community action.

The doors of the store had hardly opened when West Virginia's most celebrated politician, Robert Byrd, armed with letters from merchants and other disenchanted citizens, expressed his views concerning the store: "I have asked the U.S. Office of Economic Opportunity for a report on a cooperative grocery store that opened this month near Baisden, Mingo County. I am disturbed by reports that antipoverty funds are being used to establish businesses to be in competition with small business establishments." He further commented, "I am absolutely against this program being used to drive our business people out of business. . . . They have enough problems without additional competition resulting from efforts on the part of antipoverty workers." He refused to believe that the store had been established without the use of federal funds.

Robert Byrd was not related to the Byrds of Virginia, but many West Virginians and others felt that he belonged to Virginia or to one of the Deep South states. In his early years, he had been a member of the Ku Klux Klan, and, as a senator, he had voted against most major civil rights legislation. I was later told by an aide who had worked for Senator Robert Kennedy that Byrd was generally the mouth-piece for the Southern segregationists in the U.S. Senate.

Byrd further stated, "The war on poverty has been mis-managed, poorly administered, and wasteful with its bene-fits, often failing to reach the poor." Commenting on VISTA workers, he said:

> I don't believe these characters shipped in from other areas of the country are competent to advise our people in West Vir-ginia on how to solve their local problems. These programs in some areas have been beneficial to some extent. But, in other areas, they have constituted a haven for individuals who want to stir up strife and dissension. Too many antipoverty employees have engaged in fomenting unrest. They have in-cited welfare recipients to conduct demonstrations against the Welfare Department, public officials, and the police. Congress did not intend to appropriate money for these purposes. Con-gress shouldn't even consider a tax increase to combat infla-tion and to help finance the war in Vietnam until it trims spending for the war on poverty, foreign aid, and welfare programs.

Byrd's remarks inflamed the poor of Mingo, and they fired back. Roy Ellis said, "It sounds like he is representing Alabama rather than West Virginia. He would make Wal-lace a good running mate in '68. If the senator could find time to visit Mingo County's poor rather than huddling with local politicians who want to maintain control over us poor people, he would find that benefits are reaching the poor."

Ray Thompson complained, "It appears that Senator Byrd is opposed to free enterprise and competition, espe-cially if it comes from us poor people."

Frances Wells, a very vocal black woman from William-son, said, "I thought it was just the local politicians who were scared to death of the poverty program and the articulate poor, but it seems to me old Byrd is a little scared, too. I don't understand it. The only thing we want to do is improve ourselves, help our kids be like other kids, and have liberty and freedom. The only thing I can ever remember politicians doing is wanting to buy all the poor people's votes. I ain't got nothing for him. He's just like all the rest."

Everyone in the county knew that Byrd was a close friend of Noah's, and it was feared that this friendship could eventually wreck the poverty program. Noah always invited Byrd to the county at least once a year, and several of the high school principals invariably invited him to address the graduating classes.

By the latter part of January, the store had not been authorized to receive food stamps, and I became very concerned. If the store missed the February stamp business, it would begin to lose money. I attempted to discuss the problem with Frank DeMartino, a native of New York State who had been sent to West Virginia by the U.S. Department of Agriculture to administer the food program. But, whenever I called his office, I was told that he was on vacation or out of the office on business. Each time, I left a message for the call to be returned. It never was. Finally, my patience tried, I called the Regional Agricultural Office in New York and discussed our problem with Phillip Stern. He explained that the issuance of an authorization card was a simple process and could be done on the spot. He agreed that one month was much too long to wait. I explained that I had just called DeMartino's office and was told he was on vacation.

Stern replied, "You will get a call within fifteen minutes."

Within fifteen minutes, the call came—not from Stern but from DeMartino. "Hi, Perry, understand you have attempted to reach me."

"Yes, on several occasions. In fact, I just talked with Mr. Phillip Stern after all my attempts to get in touch with you were unsuccessful."

"What did you tell him?" He was somewhat concerned.

"I only explained to him that the community action store was having an extremely difficult time getting an authorization card and that I was unable to get up with you."

He replied, "I don't see why you told him that. You know I am very busy, having this entire state to attend to."

"I still think a month is too long to wait for a card. Besides, you never attempted to return my call."

"Well, I'll be at the store tomorrow at 10:00 A.M. Have your employees there for instruction."

DeMartino came as promised the next morning, inspected the store, and issued a conditional food stamp authorization card. The card, however, was useless because it prohibited the acceptance of food stamps as long as recipients owned corporate stock and shared in the store's profits. The conditions were based upon a vague regulation of the Department of Agriculture's that prohibited food stamp recipients from making a profit from the food stamp program. The regulation was originally intended to prevent fraud by recipients, but now it was being applied to the shareholders of the Gilbert Creek store. As a result, food stamps could not be accepted by the store until the food stamp recipients disposed of their shares. The same condition applied to the Gilbert Creek Community Action Group because its membership was made up primarily of food stamp recipients. It, too, would be required to dispose of

$2,600 in shares, which it had purchased collectively through fund-raising projects and donations. The conditions defeated the entire purpose of the store.

When I learned of these conditions, my first reaction, as I banged the top of my desk, was, "Why, that son of a bitch! How can he possibly do that? That damned Senator Byrd and Congressman Kee have gotten to him."

I immediately made several phone calls to the OEO and to the Department of Agriculture. The people at OEO said they would check with the Agriculture Secretary, and those at the Agricultural Regional Office said that they would refer the matter to their legal counsel if I would outline my complaints in writing.

It appeared that we were stymied. I knew Kee had entered the picture, for, along with Byrd, he had requested an investigation of the store. In fact, Kee was probably very much disappointed because Sargent Shriver, director of the Office of Economic Opportunity, lauded the store. In a letter to Kee, which he made public, Shriver had said:

> The cooperative grocery store organized by the poor in Mingo County is one of the best examples of community action in the war against poverty. These co-ops are the result of efforts by private groups of low income families in the economically depressed areas of West Virginia. OEO isn't involved in the financing of this store. The community action agency in Mingo, however, has provided technical guidance and advice for the project in the interest of helping the poor help themselves.

Shriver's statement had encouraged us, but now things looked bleak. I kept thinking of those special conditions that had been placed on the store, and at 3:30 P.M. (I'll never forget the moment) I had a brain storm. I buzzed

Donna and asked her to get the stock exchange in Huntington for me.

"What in the world do you want them for?"

"Never mind, you'll know later."

Once I had the exchange on the line, I inquired, "How much is A & P selling for today?"

"$27.50," answered the stockbroker.

"May I purchase one share and wire you the money?"

"Yes, sir, we would be glad to make such a transaction for you if you will give me your name."

I said, "I would like to purchase the stock in the name of the Gilbert Creek Community Action Group, Incorporated."

Thirty minutes later, the exchange called me back and confirmed the transaction. I had just purchased the last share of the day.

When I asked the secretary to get Phillip Stern on the phone again, I still had not told the other members of the staff my plan. As soon as Stern came to the phone, I informed him that the Gilbert Creek Community Action Group had just become the owner of one share of stock in A & P, thus making all A & P stores in the United States ineligible to receive food stamps.

He was nearly speechless but finally asked me to give him once again the details of the special conditions that had been attached to the food stamp authorization card and explained that he would give the matter very prompt attention.

Two days later, Frank DeMartino came and removed the special conditions from the authorization card. It was a setback for the opponents of the store. I thought of Byrd and Kee and couldn't help grinning.

9

In the summer of 1967, the Mingo County Economic Opportunity Commission granted me a leave of absence for three months to work with the OEO in the development and implementation of a neighborhood center program that involved fourteen major cities throughout the United States. During that time, I was able to compare the urban community action programs with the developments in rural Mingo County. The problems of the poor were basically the same. However, the political machines of the big-city mayors were far more sophisticated than Noah's, making them that much more difficult to deal with.

Whereas Noah had a direct line to Governor Hulett Smith and Senator Robert Byrd, many of the big-city mayors had direct lines to the White House. In many instances, one telephone call to a Presidential assistant could radically change the intent of a poverty program in a big city. Mayor Richard Daley of Chicago completely controlled the types of programs that were funded in his city. Although I was assigned responsibility for Chicago, I was instructed by the OEO not to interfere between Daley and the White House.

In fact, Chicago was really considered off limits to me. I was deeply disappointed by the OEO's inability to deal directly with the local poverty boards and by the constant pressures the White House exerted on the agency. Nevertheless, it was an extremely interesting assignment, and the three months passed quickly.

I returned to Mingo in mid-October. It felt good to be back. But I soon discovered that there was total confusion between the poor people in the county and the chairman of the EOC board, undertaker Jerry Chafin. From what the community people told me, Chafin had attempted to hire Howard Chambers, ex-sheriff and political boss of the county, as a community aide without the permission of the Board of Directors. He also had approved the Board of Education's Elementary and Secondary Education Act (ESEA) proposal without discussing it with the Board of Directors. The staff was of the opinion that Chafin had usurped his power as chairman of the board and president of the Commission and that the Commission itself, especially the poor people, should reprimand him. Calls came in from all over the county, many of them welcoming me back and many complaining about the behavior of Chafin. Several community people felt that Chafin was using the Commission to build himself a political machine. It was rumored that his father, Jeff Chafin, was planning to run for sheriff of the county, and it was assumed that Jerry would run for the Board of Education.

It was Gladoula White who suggested that we call a special meeting of all community action chairmen to discuss the problem with Jerry Chafin. I, too, felt that such action was a good idea, and I notified the other chairmen. We all agreed to meet the following Wednesday at Mrs. White's house in Lenore, a small community fifteen miles north of Williamson. At this meeting, not satisfied with his response, the chairmen of the community action groups decided to make an attempt to oust Chafin.

The by-laws had been amended recently, making all community action chairmen members of the Commission, and there was also a provision approved that allowed the Commission by a two-thirds vote to veto any decision by the Board of Directors. Because more than two-thirds of the Commission consisted of poor people, they could now control agency policy. It was also assumed that the Commission could at any time choose its own officers or reprimand a member if at least two-thirds felt that the member had overstepped his authority.

The strategy was to move fast. A special meeting of the Commission was called for the following Monday, which was five days away, to discuss Chafin's hiring of Howard Chambers and his authorized approval of the ESEA proposal. The poor had decided to test their strength, for it was believed that Jerry Chafin would rally the establishment behind him. It was a major crisis for the community action agency.

I felt as if I had never been away.

To further complicate matters, Joe Smith, Mingo County's field representative from the Office of Economic Opportunity in Washington, had recently resigned his office, so the county (and the agency) was without an experienced field representative. This could be crucial because Chafin had been able to develop some rapport with higher echelons in the regional Office of Economic Opportunity. He had also maintained a good relationship with Congressman Jim Kee. All these matters were considered, but the chairmen felt that the stakes were too high not to go ahead with the ouster proceedings.

The following Monday, the Commission met at 7:00 P.M. in the EOC office building at Cinderella. Chafin had attempted to call off the Monday night meeting by placing an article in the *Williamson Daily News* on Saturday, stating that the Commission meeting would not be held the following Monday evening, because the EOC office building was not large enough to hold the crowd. He indicated that he would call a meeting later to be held in the Appalachian Auditorium. (The EOC office building could seat 150 people; the Appalachian Auditorium, only about 75.) Evidently, Chafin had received word that he was going to be ousted by the Commission, and, therefore, he was making an effort to postpone the meeting. The only members of the Commission who appeared that night were the chairmen of the community action groups. However, there were more than enough for a quorum. So the meeting was called to order, and Dr. H. D. Clarke, chairman of the local chapter of the NAACP and a member of the Vinson Street Community Action Group, was called upon to conduct the meeting because he was serving as vice-president of the Commission.

Robert Curry, the OEO's brand new field representative, arrived at 6:00. I had called him on Sunday and explained to him the situation that had developed in Mingo, and I was hopeful that he would understand. I had met Curry once while I was working in Washington. He was a Presbyterian minister who had originally worked in a youth program in Washington, D.C., was in his late thirties, and had no previous experience in community action. He indicated that he would accept the decision of the Commission, especially as this Commission meeting was composed entirely of low income people, with the exception of Dr. Clarke.

Together, Bob and I reread the EOC by-laws to determine whether the Commission had the right to oust Chafin. Although there were no provisions that defined ouster proceedings, at least two sections indicated that the Commission had the right to determine its own course of action and to select its own officers at any time. Although neither Bob nor I felt that the legal counsel of the mid-Atlantic regional office of the OEO would go along with the decision of the Commission to oust Chafin, we felt that, at least, the Office of Economic Opportunity would eventually have to intervene in the matter and make a final decision. It would be interesting to see whether it agreed to uphold a decision made by the poor or whether it would back away and uphold the faction headed by Jerry Chafin.

After the Commission meeting was called to order, Bob Belcher, community action chairman from Chattaroy, was the first to speak. Looking straight at Dr. Clarke, Belcher stated, "It is my opinion that this here Chafin fellow has certainly overstepped his power. I would like to ask this Commission how he had the authority to hire Howard Chambers and to sign off on the ESEA proposal without first bringing it before the Board of Directors of the Commission. Now, I've been told, and I don't know whether it's true, but at least I've been told that this Commission here is supposed to attend to its own affairs, and it's supposed to be a democratic process, and one man is not supposed to make the decisions for this Commission. Now, if this is the case, and I feel it is, then I feel that Chafin has overstepped his authority, and I think this Commission should get to the bottom of it. I spend a lot of time down in the streets of Williamson, and I've been hearing a lot of rumors that Chafin is attempting to use this organization to build himself a political machine. I don't think we can tolerate this kind of thinking on the Commission, nor can this Commission afford to be controlled by one-man rule."

Dr. Clarke interrupted, "Is that all you have to say, brother? Then I'll recognize Mrs. Gladoula White."

Mrs. White, a former welfare recipient, had been working with the Head Start Program as a teacher's aide. She and Lewis, her husband, had received $53 a month before the poverty program came to Mingo. "Mr. Chairman," she said, "I feel we have no other course of action other than to ask for the immediate removal of Mr. Chafin as president of this Commission and chairman of the Board of Directors."

Several of the Commission members agreed openly.

Dr. Clarke interrupted, "Mrs. White, do you put that in the form of a motion?"

"Yes, I do."

"Is there other discussion concerning the motion that's on the floor to oust Jerry Chafin as president of the Commission and chairman of the Board of Directors?"

One Commission member after another stood and stated his reasons for supporting the ouster of Chafin. After about forty minutes, the vote was taken, and, of the thirty-three Commission members present, thirty-two voted to remove Chafin from office.

The Commission also removed three other members, because they had missed three consecutive meetings. Four additional members were replaced because they were no longer chairmen of their local community action groups. As a result, seven replacements were made on the Commission.

After the meeting, Curry and I went to my office and discussed what had taken place. Curry, grinning and looking over his glasses, said, "Perry, you bastard, you're gonna get me fired in Washington before I get started. I don't know if what we did tonight was legal, but I'll tell you one thing, it was a beautiful sight to see poor people standing up for their own rights. It's a damn shame that some of the other community action agencies throughout the country don't conduct their business like Mingo." He shook his head. "Those people really know what they want, and Jerry Chafin or the OEO isn't going to stop them from getting it."

I replied, "I think you're right, Bob. I think what happened tonight was really a display of 'poor power.' What you witnessed is what happens when poor people are organized. They are no longer going to allow middle-class establishments to tell them what they can do and what they can't do. They are truly a representative voice of the poor."

"By the way, Perry, what do you think Chafin's next move will be?"

"I believe he'll call a meeting of the Board of Directors. You know, Bob, the structure of this organization is highly unusual—having the Commission that has certain authorities and then having a Board of Directors with certain authorities. It confuses the situation. I would imagine that Chafin will call a board meeting, and the directors, being primarily establishment people, will probably back Chafin. However, I'm not sure that he can get a quorum. Of course, the one thing that protects the poor is that they can veto any decision of the board by a two-thirds majority vote. Certainly, tonight's meeting has put the board and Chafin on the defensive. I think we will continue to move ahead and conduct business in accordance with the decisions and the desires of the Commission, and overlook the Board of Directors entirely."

Curry said, "O.K. Well, I've got to get the hell out of here and get back to Charleston and catch a plane to Washington. I'll call you tomorrow."

The following day, the headline on the front page of the *Williamson Daily News read*, "Gerald Chafin Removed as President of the Mingo EOC." The article explained the reasons for the dismissal of Chafin. And, just as I had predicted to Curry, Chafin called a meeting of the Board of Directors of the EOC for 7:30 Wednesday evening in the Appalachian Power Company Auditorium.

I called a staff meeting of all the project directors and the immediate central office staff to discuss the situation. The consensus was that, if Jerry Chafin was allowed to control the antipoverty program in Mingo County, it would become just an ordinary poverty program like the rest in West Virginia. There was strong determination to prevent this situation from occurring, and the entire staff threw its support behind the Commission members.

On Wednesday evening, when the Board of Directors met with Jerry, all the community action chairmen boycotted the meeting. The poor had no representatives in attendance, and, consequently, the only knowledge they had of what happened was what they read in the *Williamson Daily News*. On Thursday, under the headline "Squabble over Mingo E.O.C. Is Headed for Washington, Directors Back Gerald Chafin," the paper said:

> The inner turmoil among officers, directors, and members of the Mingo County Economic Opportunity Commission has reached the point where the powers that be at the Office of Economic Opportunity in the Nation's Capital are being asked to set the matter of command.

The question of whether he is or isn't the President of the Mingo E.O.C. hovered around Gerald L. Chafin of Delbarton today. Although a quorum of Commission Directors last night gave him a vote of confidence as head of the group, there was further controversy over Huey Perry of Gilbert who returned to Williamson last week to assume his duties as Director of the Mingo E.O.C. The E.O.C. Board of Directors meeting last night in the Appalachian Auditorium said in effect that Perry is not an employee of the E.O.C. at present and would not be until he presented his desires before the Board for its action.

After much discussion by the Board last night, the group voted to turn over three sets of the Commission by-laws and a copy of the E.O.C. minutes to Robert Curry, an O.E.O. field representative. Curry is to submit these to the O.E.O. in Washington, D. C. Chafin told the *Daily News* this morning that the Board of Directors voted to call a special Board meeting on November 7 at 7:30 p.m. in the Appalachian Auditorium in the expectation that a decision would be received from the Washington O.E.O. Office.

Last night's meeting had been postponed from Monday night although thirty-four Commission members went ahead with a meeting on that night in the E.O.C. offices at Cinderella. The Monday night group voted to remove Chafin from office for a series of acts beyond his authority.

As the matter stood today, Chafin appeared to remain as President by authority of the E.O.C. Board of Directors who met last night, while Dr. H. D. Clarke, first vice-president of the E.O.C., was recognized by the group of Commission members who met Monday night as the acting president until the annual election next February. The Monday night group also approved the reinstatement of Perry as Director of the Commission, but the Board of Directors meeting last night recognizes only that Larry Hamrick is still acting director until such time as Perry appears before the Board to request reinstatement.

I called Robert Curry and explained to him what had happened and read to him the above and additional paragraphs from the newspaper account. He informed me that he was already aware of what had happened, and he said that he wanted to call a special meeting of all the Commission members, and also that he would bring down Ed Cogen, the deputy director for the mid-Atlantic region; Len Slaughter, the district director for West Virginia; and the OEO legal counsel to attend it. He also said that Chafin had been on the phone to Ed Cogen during the day, that he was somewhat afraid of what Ed Cogen might do regarding the situation, and that Congressman Kee's office had called. There was the possibility that Congressman Kee would intervene and exert pressure upon the regional office to go along with Chafin rather than with the poor.

The following day, I learned that Chafin, Ralph Vinciguerra, and Tilda Sepich had been invited to Washington by Ed Cogen to discuss the Mingo situation. This was certainly bad news for the poor people in the county. It now appeared that the OEO would go along with Chafin rather than with the poor. In a phone conversation with Ed Cogen, I voiced my dissatisfaction. However, he indicated that it was necessary to bring Chafin and the group to Washington to determine what their complaints were. He indicated that his boss, Leveo Sanchez, the regional director, was under considerable pressure from Congressman Kee's office. He also reminded me that the poverty program was being debated before the House and that an unpleasant situation developing in Mingo could perhaps hurt the chances of the poverty bill's being passed in Congress. Certainly, the supporters of the bill did not want to lose Congressman Kee's vote; they felt that it was crucial to get every vote possible. I told Cogen in rather angry language that the poverty bill certainly was not worth a damn if it had to respond to the establishment rather than to the poor and that I felt it was time the OEO got off its ass and quit worrying about Congress and began to worry once and for all about the poor people for which it was intended.

On Monday, November 4, I was directed by Robert Curry to set up a meeting of all the Commission members. The OEO had finally decided to come to Mingo, and it had established the ground rule that no business would be conducted at this meeting. The meeting was to be for information only.

That evening, Jeff Monroe, the state technical assistance director, came to Mingo, along with Len Slaughter, Cogen, Bob Curry, and Les Minkus. Minkus was the OEO attorney, who probably would make the final decision on the legality of removing Chafin from the presidency of the Commission.

Monroe, like Robert Curry, was a Presbyterian minister. He had been the state technical assistance director for several months and was a strong advocate of community organization and involvement of the poor in all decision-making. For what good it was, he was clearly on the side of the poor people in Mingo. I was hopeful that he could influence, or at least assist in the influencing of, the decisions of the OEO in Washington. In my private conversations with Monroe, I indicated that I felt that he would be most helpful if he could have some private discussion with Minkus, and especially Cogen. He indicated that he would, after the meeting.

The staff and I had met with the community action chairmen the previous evening, and I had attempted to bring them up to date as much as possible on the developments that were taking place. However, it was a difficult job when events were developing so quickly, especially with a government bureaucracy such as the OEO. One thing for sure, however: The poor were prepared to boycott the anti-poverty program in Mingo if the OEO overruled their decision to oust Jerry Chafin.

More than three hundred people jammed the old Cinderella coal company building. It undoubtedly was the largest crowd that had ever been inside the EOC office. There was an air of tenseness, especially among the poor, for they knew they would have to present a convincing case to the OEO officials before the officials could understand the situation.

Chafin, wearing a dark blue mortician's suit and his familiar black derby, arrived at 6:30. He immediately shook hands with Ed Cogen and Les Minkus, smiling broadly all the time.

Curry, being as honest as he could with me, told me that he did not know what the final outcome would be, but he, too, was somewhat confused by the attitude of Cogen and Les Minkus. He assumed, as I did, that a great deal of pressure was being exerted by Congressman Kee's office and that we would have to present a strong case if we were to convince the OEO.

A small table was pulled to the front of the room, and the four representatives from the OEO and Chafin sat down. It was now 7:05. Chafin stood, laid his gold watch on the table along with his pipe, and said, "This meeting is now called to order."

Emerson Jarrell, a wiry, middle-aged man dressed in faded bib overalls, rose to his feet and challenged Chafin: "Mr. Chafin, let me tell you one thing right now. You are not going to preside over this meeting tonight. We ousted you, and therefore, we are not going to allow you to preside over a meeting of this Commission."

This caught the OEO officials off guard. It also startled Chafin. He looked around to Cogen. "What do you propose, Mr. Cogen?"

Cogen certainly was startled. He did not want to get involved in this kind of decision so early in the meeting. He looked somewhat puzzled and did not make any reply to Chafin.

Chafin continued, "In a meeting of the Board of Directors, I was given a vote of confidence."

This was as far as he got. Jarrell interrupted again. "I don't care what the Board of Directors gave you, Chafin; you are not going to preside over this meeting, and, if you attempt to preside over it, we, as a Commission, and every one of us that attended the Monday night meeting where you were ousted will get up and walk out of the meeting."

In unity, all of the community action chairmen chimed in, "That's right!"

Cogen, sensing that there was a good possibility that there would not be a meeting at all, intervened. He explained why he and the other members of the OEO were there and why they had originally called the meeting. He said, "We in the OEO want to understand all the facts behind this situation and behind the problem in Mingo County. This is why we have come to the county—to hear both sides of the argument. I do not see, personally, why it matters who presides over this meeting."

Again, Jarrell, the spokesman, interrupted. "Mr. Cogen, it may not matter to you, but it matters to us. It's a matter of principle, and we do not intend for that man," pointing to Jerry Chafin, "to preside over a meeting of this Commission after we went to the trouble of ousting him at our last regular Commission meeting."

Almost twenty minutes had passed, and the poor were

holding to their contention that Chafin would not preside over the meeting. Finally, Cogen asked whether he could preside. Chafin agreed to step aside and allow Cogen to conduct the meeting.

I was sitting on the steps of the balcony that overlooked the meeting place. I was extremely pleased with the position that the community action chairmen had taken and felt immediately that they had won a psychological victory by making Chafin step aside.

Cogen went on to explain the principles of the war on poverty and the problems in Mingo as he viewed them. "We are hopeful that you people can come together tonight and resolve this conflict that exists between you. We are aware that there are three sets of by-laws that are conflicting. We are also aware that the minutes of the Commission are not always clear as to what has taken place."

Although Cogen did not realize it, he was turning off many poor people. They were in no mood to compromise with the establishment, as I had tried to explain to him prior to the meeting. However, he had not listened, obviously feeling that the best road to solving the problems of Mingo was through compromise. Compromise was what the poor were not willing to accept, but Chafin was well satisfied with the way Cogen was conducting the meeting. On two or three occasions, he looked around and smiled nonchalantly, as if he were under no pressure at all. Many of the Commission members were becoming infuriated with Cogen's talk. Several of them turned and looked at me as if to say they could not believe what the OEO was actually saying, for they viewed Ed Cogen as the OEO.

Lewis White, the husband of Gladoula, was the first to speak out against Cogen. A life-long resident of Mingo

County, Lewis had suffered through the Depression, had lost his health, and was totally disabled from working in the mines. He had been beaten out of his miner's welfare and also his Social Security. Lewis was extremely grateful for what the war on poverty had been able to accomplish in Mingo. He had been sitting on the steps leading up to the balcony. He rose to his feet, walked to the front of the table, interrupted Cogen's speech, and pointed his finger directly at him.

"Let me tell you something right now, Mr. OEO. It sounds to me like you ain't a bit better off than the politicians in Mingo County. Now, I want to tell you one thing right now, and I want you to listen, young man. If you've come down here to give this poverty program back to the politicians, you can take your goddamned money and put it in your little black bag and take it back to Washington. We're not gonna bow down to damn politicians any longer, nor are we gonna bow down to you. And it sounds to me like you've come down here to tell us to get back in bed with these damn politicians, and that we're not gonna do. Just look at 'em; they don't even want to hire Huey Perry back as the director, and he's the damn best director in the country. Why, you fellers up in Washington had to even call him up there to come and help you out. Now, he might not like what I'm saying about him here now, but there's not a damn thing he can do about it either."

Cogen sat back down in his chair and leaned far back in his seat.

"Now, that's all I've gotta say to you. If you go along with them damned politicians, you just take your damned money, put it in your black bag, and go back to Washington. That's all. I've made my point."

Cogen finally concluded the meeting by telling the Commission that the OEO office would study the by-laws and would make some recommendations to the Commission within the next two days.

Robert Curry followed me back to my office after the meeting. I entered first, and Bob closed the door behind him. He shook my hand and said, "Perry, I think they did it out there. Lewis White was a beautiful man. If Cogen didn't get that message, then there's no way of communicating with him. I really think that did it."

"I sure hope so, Bob," was all I could think to say.

Two days later, I received a telegram from the OEO mid-Atlantic regional office, signed by Leveo Sanchez, the regional director. It stated that the grant documents of the Mingo County EOC had been reviewed and that it had been determined that a special condition requiring seven changes in the by-laws had not been met by August 1, 1967, as required. Therefore, the EOC was directed to make the changes and submit the amended by-laws to the federal agency for approval. Until such time as this was done, any and all actions of the Commission or board taken on the authority of the unamended sections of the by-laws could not be recognized by the agency. Sanchez's telegram stated that six amendments to the by-laws must be made. The most important change would allow the Commission to veto a decision of the Board of Directors by a two-thirds majority vote. (It was heartening that the OEO had recognized the importance of a set of by-laws that gave the veto power to the Commission. Although the by-laws the Commission was using as a guide already contained the veto provision, the OEO felt it should be acted upon again because this was the provision Chafin refused to recognize.)

Of equal importance was the question concerning the filling of vacancies as they occurred on the Board. The OEO directed in the telegram that the vacancies should be filled by the Commission rather than by the Board. This would take a considerable amount of power away from the Chafin faction. The other required amendments were minor in relation to the conflict between the Commission and Jerry Chafin. But, until the amendments were made, the OEO was not recognizing any actions taken by either the Board of Directors or the Commission since August 1. It referred primarily to events that had occurred at the meeting of the Commission on October 23 and the meeting of the Board of Directors on October 25.

After studying the telegram, we concluded that, once the amendments to the by-laws were made, the Commission, or the chairmen of the community action groups that were represented on the Commission, could do legally what it had already done.

Seizing the initiative from Chafin, we worked out the drafts for the by-laws amendments, mailed them to all Commission members, and called for a special meeting to amend the by-laws.

During the next seven days, there was much anxiety about the future of the antipoverty program in Mingo. Small strategy meetings were held each night to make sure everyone understood his role in the upcoming meeting and, above all, to make sure everyone was provided with transportation to the meeting.

Chafin and his supporters were also holding meetings to enlist support from other organizations and people who were disenchanted with the antipoverty activities.

As expected, the building was packed to capacity on the

evening of the meeting. Newspaper reporters scurried through the crowd asking questions and jotting down notes. People were chattering in little groups all around the room. Others hung over the balcony that overlooked the meeting room. It was almost like a courtroom atmosphere with everyone awaiting the decision of the jury.

As Chafin rapped his gavel to convene the meeting, the crowd quieted. The community action chairmen sat patiently awaiting their chance to speak.

The first clash involved the seating of two women on the Commission who had previously been removed for failure to attend meetings. Both were strong supporters of Chafin. However, the community action chairmen held their ground and prevented them from being seated.

Other procedural questions were brought up by Ralph Vinciguerra, the elementary school principal who had accompanied Chafin to Washington. Each time, he was shouted down by Emerson Jarrell, who had previously challenged Vinciguerra's membership on the Commission.

I sat impatiently on the stairs leading up to the balcony. It was evident that the meeting was going to drag on and on as the Chafin forces continued to argue over procedure.

Finally, after losing all patience with Vinciguerra because of his long dissertations on by-laws and procedures, Jarrell jumped to his feet and once again challenged Vinciguerra's membership on the Commission.

"On what basis?" Chafin asked.

"What basis? That Vinciguerra has not been a member of the Gilbert Kiwanis Club for almost a year and a half." Pointing his finger at Vinciguerra, Jarrell continued, "You haven't attended the Kiwanis Club meetings for a year and a half, and you've been sitting on the Commission illegally representing the Kiwanis Club. You were reinstated only five weeks ago."

Mr. Vinciguerra replied, "Oh, no!"

"Mr. Jarrell, we have no letter from the Kiwanis Club stating that Mr. Vinciguerra is not a member of the Commission, and, until such time, he will remain on the Commission," said Chafin.

"Is there a member of the Gilbert Kiwanis Club present here tonight?" Jarrell asked.

Vinciguerra interrupted, "Mr. Jarrell, I'll give you all the information you need, sir. You just got through saying that I paid my dues five weeks ago."

Mr. Jarrell retaliated, "I said that you were only reinstated five weeks ago."

"Well, that's all right. I paid my dues, didn't I?" Vinciguerra was angry.

Jarrell replied, "Yes, but you was out for a year and a half up until that time, though."

Vinciguerra shouted, "What about presently? I'm presently a member of that organization."

Jarrell interrupted. "You were throwed out and reinstated five weeks ago, and you sat on this board illegally."

Vinciguerra countered, "Mr. Jarrell, I was waiting for you to hang yourself with a bit of rope, but I'll just not do it. I'll just take you off the hook. About a year and a half ago—to be exact, August last year—I began teaching at night, on Tuesday night. That's the night that the Kiwanis meets, and I was permitted to miss those meetings because of that. And of course now—"

The telephone rang. Robert Curry was calling from Washington. The telephone was located in the center of the room, on a small table. During the day, it was on the

129

reception desk. The other furniture had been moved away to make room for the meeting. Ray Thompson from the Gilbert Creek Community Action Group answered the phone and motioned for me.

I had talked with Curry before the meeting, and I knew in advance he was going to call at 7:30 P.M. The meeting was interrupted during our conversation while I explained to Curry, in the presence of everyone, what was happening. Chafin and Vinciguerra were infuriated by the call and even more so when I reported Curry's comment that the Commission could oust a member by a majority vote.

After I sat down, Vinciguerra said, "Mr. President, I wouldn't worry too much about what Robert Curry said. I've been to three meetings, and that's the first time that he's ever opened his mouth to say anything. I wouldn't worry about what he says even if he is from Washington. But I'll tell you one thing, as sure as certain, on my way down here this evening—I came by myself, and I said to myself, 'Surely the people on that Commission are honest people, and they'd like to see the honest thing done. I'd hate to think I'm associated with so many people who are not honest.' I said, 'Well, they're bound to be honest. They're bound to be working for the right thing; they have their own minds and can do their own thinking.' I was hoping that I was associated with that type of people rather than a group of people who would let someone put words in their mouth and so forth. And, if you're that type, I feel sorry for you. I'll tell you one thing: You can't operate this program without others. You just can't do it; it's impossible. It's impossible, and I think the more you cooperate with others, the better off you are.

"Mr. President, I would like to ask one question. I would

like to know why it is that just certain people—" He stopped in an effort to collect himself and then proceeded. "They're just trying to keep certain people off this Commission, and I was highly interested in this research that Mr. Jarrell made concerning my membership in the Gilbert Kiwanis Club. Did you go over there, Mr. Jarrell, and get that information? Is that reliable information that you have?"

Several community chairmen other than Jarrell chimed in, but it was Jarrell who answered. "Well, we're going to vote you out, and, if you are eligible, then we'll put you back in. But the information that we received is reliable information, and it indicates that you are not eligible to serve on this Commission."

Observing that Vinciguerra was on the verge of being removed from the Commission, Chafin quickly changed the tone of the meeting and began reading the new amendments to the by-laws. It was a time-consuming process, and, altogether, an hour passed before the final amendment was approved. The poor people were now in control of the poverty agency. However, this did not prevent the ensuing arguments concerning membership. Chafin and his supporters would not agree that the Commission could oust a member. The community action chairmen contended that it did have that power.

During the arguments over this issue, Robert Curry once again called and reaffirmed that the Commission had the right to select its own membership. I once again explained this fact to the Commission.

Vinciguerra angrily charged, "Perry is calling all the shots, and he's not even a member of this Commission."

O. T. Kent took the floor again and said, "Mr. Chairman,

I don't see how we can get orders out of Washington by telephone when last week we had four of them sitting here with their lawyer, and they couldn't tell us anything. Everything we'd ask them, they'd say, 'We're not down here to tell you; we're not butting into your business.' You'd ask them a direct question, and they couldn't answer it. They would evade the question every time. And now, you call up Washington and get a direct answer on anything you want. And I can't see how they do it, when we sat right in here with four of them and their lawyer, and they couldn't tell us anything. They refused to answer question after question. 'It's your business down here. You do this, and you do that. We don't butt into your business.' Then you get on the telephone here, and they tell us what to do. I don't like it a bit."

One of the Commission members countered, "Mr. Kent, that's exactly what we're trying to do—take care of our own business."

At this point, Robert Belcher, chairman of the Chattaroy Community Action Group, took the floor and said that he believed the Commission should oust all members who were not in good standing with it.

Vinciguerra interrupted, "Mr. Chairman, I have no intentions of trying to prove that I should be on this Commission. I'm a duly elected representative of an authorized organization that was invited to send an elected representative to sit on this organization. I'm a dues-paying member of that organization, in good standing, and, as you indicated, I have not withdrawn as a representative of that organization, and I'm not going to defend myself because they don't want me on this Commission, and that's perfectly all right with me. It's perfectly all right. But I just wanted to get the facts straight. That's all I'm interested in. And then, if the Commission wants to vote me out, that's all right. I don't object at all. But, Mr. Chairman, while I have the floor, and I'm still a duly recognized member of the Commission, I'd like for you to inform these people, who are so anxious to know everything that's going on, of all the facts and figures that you took up to Mr. Sanchez and tell them what you have learned about what's going on here in this EOC office."

What information Chafin had taken to Washington was anyone's guess. Vinciguerra's argument only tended to make the community action members angry with him, especially as he went on to indicate that he knew more about what was going on than the other members of the Commission knew.

"I make it a point to know. I don't mean that I'm smarter; I've just made it a point to exercise my position on the Board of Directors. But, if they can honestly, and I mean this, from the bottom of my heart, if they who made these motions, who are interested in ousting me, if they can face their maker tonight when they go home and say, 'I'm sincere in getting rid of Ralph Vinciguerra,' then more power to them. But, if you don't, I feel sorry for you. I feel sorry for you. You don't even know me, and then you feel that way; you are letting somebody lead you. I feel sorry for you. I think it's too bad myself.

"Mr. Chairman, I would like to suggest that they go ahead and vote as to whether I'm a member of this Commission. If they're gonna vote, let them vote, and, if they don't want me, that'll be all right. I'll step aside—be glad! I would like a roll call vote. Put it to a vote."

Chafin requested that Jarrell restate his motion.

Vinciguerra interrupted again: "And I want everyone to know what the reasons are that they're ousting me, for my lack of being qualified."

As he sat down, the roll call vote began, and it was soon evident that he would be ousted. The final vote was thirty to six to remove Vinciguerra. The other members in question were also removed by the same vote count.

At 10:00 P.M., Hayes Stanley asked for permission to speak. "I would like to make the following motion: that Gerald Chafin be removed as president of the Commission and chairman of the Board of Directors."

Chafin, realizing that he was badly defeated, somberly asked, "Is there a second?"

Herb Meade said, "I second the motion."

The vote was taken, and Chafin turned and handed the gavel to Dr. Clarke. As he left, he was followed by Kent, Vinciguerra, Sepich, and several other supporters. All appeared to be dejected because of the Commission's decisions.

It had been a long meeting, and everyone was tired. It had taken three years for the poor to gain control of their own poverty program. After tonight, Chafin's other supporters would never attend a meeting of the Commission, and there would be no interference from them. The prospect of the poverty agency's being directed by the poor for whom it was intended was exciting. Now the poor could organize for the purpose of destroying the Noah Floyd political machine and attempt to replace it with a county government that would be responsive to their needs. If this could be accomplished, it would establish a precedent in West Virginia, and perhaps people from other counties would rise up in protest against the political tyrants who controlled their lives. The strategy was to direct the energies of the poor away from development and implementation of federal programs, which usually treated only the symptoms of poverty, toward the building of a political base from which the poor could attack poverty itself.

10

No sooner had the poor people of Mingo County settled accounts with Chafin than they became involved in a bitter struggle with the county political establishment. Since the AFDCU public hearing, there had been constant quarreling between the poor people and the Floyd machine. Almost everyone anticipated a showdown. It was in preparation for this inevitable conflict that the community action agency organized the Mingo County Fair Elections Committee. Mingo had long since had the reputation of being the most corrupt county in the state. *Look* magazine described it as the "vote fraud center of the world." The greatest obstacle to the elimination of poverty in Mingo was the political machine, which manipulated elections to maintain control.

I can recall my father's talking of the many devious methods that were used in Mingo County elections in the 1920's and 1930's, when he was active in politics. He had served as a deputy sheriff under Greenway Hatfield, who was a close relative of "Devil" Anse Hatfield's, the clan leader. My father told of one election precinct where mine ponies, all of which had names, of course, were actually voted. He also told a story about a black woman of the same precinct who changed clothes three times, and each time voted under a different name. It was always customary to vote dead people.

On a Sunday in November, 1967, several EOC staff members and poor people from Mingo attended a conference held at Concord College in Athens, West Virginia, sponsored by antipoverty agencies throughout southern West Virginia and the Appalachian Volunteers, a group of community organizers financed by the OEO to assist the poor in southern West Virginia and eastern Kentucky. The item on the agenda that caught their interest most was the workshop on elections.

John Callebs, a tall, lean Marshall University professor, one of the first West Virginians to call attention to the unsavory practices of vote fraud in the state, had been invited to the workshop, and his primary attention that day was focused upon the corrupt practices in southern West Virginia counties. He charged that in eight counties alone there were 25,132 more names on the registration books than the actual population twenty-one years of age and older, as recorded in the 1960 census. He further stated that Mingo County's population of twenty-one years and older, according to the census, was 19,879; the actual number registered to vote was 30,331, just a few percentage points below the *total* population of the county.

For James Washington, this vote fraud seminar was his first community action meeting. Although he had been following the activities of the community action groups in the county in the local newspapers, he had made no effort to become involved. Washington, a fifty-one-year-old Negro widower, supported his five children on a $45-a-month vet-eran's pension and a welfare check. He had had a heart attack in the 1950's while working in a coal mine.

Upon returning from Concord College, James Washington and other members of the group who had attended the meeting began to study the West Virginia election laws, comparing them to what was actually happening in Mingo County. Washington soon found an ally in Okey Ray Spence, who was forty years old and white. Okey had been a coal miner for eighteen years, until he was forced to leave Mingo when the mines began shutting down. He went to work in Ohio in a truck assembly plant. There, in 1960, a hoist broke, dropping a truck body on him. Since then, he had been living on Social Security for the disabled and had raised a few head of livestock at his home at the head of a small hollow near Delbarton.

With the help of EOC staff and VISTA volunteers, James Washington and Okey Ray Spence began enlisting other disgruntled county voters to the cause, and soon a fair elec-tions movement was in full swing throughout the county. Small workshop meetings, with James and Okey explaining the basic election laws and comparing them to the viola-tions, were conducted at each community action group meeting everywhere in the county. Although corrupt elec-tions and corrupt politicians had been discussed freely in almost all the community action meetings during the last year, this was the first organized attempt by the poor to effect corrective measures.

The poor were aware that the delegates who were elected to go to Charleston to represent the county in the state leg-islature were controlled by the large absentee landowners and by large utility companies. Many of the local politicians received financial support from the large coal companies, from utility companies, and from the absentee landowners, who were concerned primarily with the amount of local taxes that they would be assessed. Noah, for example, was paid $6,000 a year as secretary of the Mingo County Taxpayers Association, which was financed by large coal companies and other large industries. In effect, this made Noah a lobbyist for the rich. If the fair elections effort were successful, it could deal a severe blow to the corrupt political process in the county and state.

With each meeting, enthusiasm grew, and, within sixty days from the time of the Concord conference, over two hundred poor people were participating in the work of the newly created Mingo County Fair Elections Committee, with James Washington and Okey Ray Spence as their co-chairmen. The first step was to attempt to eliminate the padded registration rolls. Election law books were ordered from the office of the Secretary of State and distributed to key members of the committee. Fortunately, the West Virginia election law contained a provision that expedited their work. This provision gave eligible voters the right to challenge other voters' rights to be registered and spelled out the procedure by which to make the challenges.

After lists of voters registered in Mingo County had been secured, district workers were recruited to check the names and mark off those they knew to be ineligible. This procedure was followed in all eight magisterial districts. The second step was to have registered voters who were interested in fair elections come to the Mingo County courthouse and fill out a challenge form at the office of the county clerk. State law requires the county clerk then to send a registered letter to the challenged voter stating that his right to be a registered voter had been challenged and that he must appear in the circuit clerk's office within a reasonable time or his name would be eliminated from the registration rolls. If the challenged voter fails to appear in the courthouse, or if the letter is returned unclaimed, it is the clerk's obligation under the law to remove the name from the rolls. The Fair Elections Committee also ordered ten sample voting machines from a New York firm, which manufactured the ones used in Mingo. At the same time that the poor were learning about the election laws, they could also learn how to use the voting machines without assistance.

Week after week, the Fair Elections Committee pushed forward toward its objectives and continued to gain support from the county's poor. By February, 1968, it had actively begun to challenge the rights of people to be registered. Groups of names were now being challenged daily, and accounts of the activities of the committee were being carried regularly in the local paper and also the state's leading paper, the *Charleston Gazette*.

Noah and other political figures in the state knew that the EOC was the primary supporting force behind the efforts of the Fair Elections Committee. Complaints were lodged through the politicians' Washington ally, Robert Byrd, who immediately made an inquiry through the Office of Economic Opportunity. I explained that the effort was nonpartisan. There were no regulations that prohibited this type of political activity.

By early March, the effects of the deregistration campaign began to show results. Members of the political machine were remarking throughout the county that the Fair Elections Committee was challenging people's rights to vote. Gradually they began to challenge openly the Fair

Elections Committee's activities. Soon, anonymous phone calls were being made to James, Okey, and me, threatening our lives if we continued with our activities. Each time, the threats were reported to the local sheriff's department and the local office of the state police. However, no efforts were made to investigate the threatening calls. Actually, no one expected either the sheriff's office or the state police to conduct an investigation; both were integral parts of the local political machine.

Although no VISTA volunteers or Appalachian Volunteers were directly involved in the challenging of voters, rumors spread rapidly throughout the county that the entire movement was inspired by the "outside dirty communists." To destroy the effectiveness of the Fair Elections Committee, the politicians also began to spread rumors throughout the county that they were going to take over the Mingo County EOC and operate the poverty agency themselves, beginning on February 1, 1969.

In 1967, Edith Green, congresswoman from Oregon and member of the Health, Education, and Welfare Committee, which is responsible for drafting amendments to the Economic Opportunity Act, managed to get an amendment passed that would allow county courts to become community action agencies, provided that the Office of Economic Opportunity concurred in the designation. Although we had not issued any public statements concerning the Green Amendment, we knew very well that there was a probability that the County Court could legally become the community action agency by February. Several of the community leaders who had been engaged in community action since its inception felt that it might be unwise to continue the activities of the Fair Elections Committee, fearing that

141

the County Court and the political machine would use the committee as an excuse to take over the agency. However, they were in the minority, and the Fair Elections Committee continued to press forward.

In early March, nine members of the committee were arrested by constables and deputy sheriffs on warrants charging them with, maliciously or frivolously and without probable cause, challenging the rights of individuals to vote, on the basis of citizen's complaints from individuals who had been challenged. The first two arrested were Lerly Murphy of Matewan and Alma Jean Justice of Gilbert. Mrs. Murphy's husband, Sidney Murphy, was a candidate for county clerk. He was endorsed by the communtiy action groups and was running as a reform candidate. Mrs. Justice, a mother of seven, was arrested at her home on March 13, after she and other members of the Fair Elections Committee in Stafford District had challenged more than 450 names. Hearings were set before local justices of the peace, although according to West Virginia law justices of the peace have no authority in matters pertaining to elections; however, it was anticipated that these officials would ignore the law and attempt to sentence the workers.

Cleo Jones, a Charleston attorney and member of the House of Delegates, was immediately questioned about the warrants. He assured the Fair Elections Committee that he would be present at the hearings, although he felt that the only solution to the matter would be to appeal to the Circuit Court. He urged the Fair Elections Committee to continue its expurgation of the public registration rolls and assured it that the warrants that had been issued were faulty and would not hold up in a court of law.

If the politicians felt that this scare method would stop

the deregistration drive, they were badly mistaken. After the arrests, Chairman James Washington issued a statement to the *Williamson Daily News*: "Our Committee is more committed than ever in its effort to insure fair elections for once in Mingo County. There isn't enough space in the Mingo County jails to hold the people willing to fight for fair elections."

He explained that the challenges had been made on legal grounds and that the only people who had been challenged were in one of four categories: (1) nonresidents in the voting precinct or district (the West Virginia election law specifically stated that a voter was ineligible to vote if he lived outside a precinct or district wherein he was registered), (2) wrong information on the permanent registration card, (3) deceased persons who had continued to vote, (4) out-of-state residents voting in Mingo County.

Washington further reported that the challenged names included those of several people who had died. In one instance, a man was challenged who had voted in every election for the past forty years although a death certificate on file in the circuit clerk's office indicated that the man had died forty years ago. The committee so far had information to indicate that more than thirty deceased persons had voted in the last general election. Washington said he had known that it was bad, but it wasn't until he started really looking into the situation that he found out how bad it was.

The county official charged with keeping the voting registration books up to date was Tom C. Chafin, the elected county clerk and the strongest critic of the Fair Elections Committee. Chafin, a grandson of the first Hatfield killed by a McCoy in Mingo County's most famous feud, had been involved in politics since he was a young man. Before he was elected to the position of county clerk, he had served as a justice of the peace in Magnolia District. When interviewed by an out-of-state newspaperman about the activities of the Fair Elections Committee, Chafin charged, "I think it is the 'Unfair Elections Committee.' We were doing a good job on voter registration. We have the best registration this county has ever had, and I have always enforced the letter of the law in Mingo."

The reporter countered, "But the law says, for instance, that a voter must be registered to vote in the precinct in which he votes, and the Fair Elections Committee has challenged many voters on this question."

Chafin was angered by this statement. He said, "Down through the years, people have been voting in whatever precinct they want. If you lived in precinct four and you wanted to vote in precinct five, I don't see what is wrong with that—just so you only vote once."

Asked if he knew of any dead people who had voted recently in Mingo County elections, Chafin answered, "If there was ever a deceased person voted, I'd sure like to see it. Let them put up or shut up!"

Chafin was so convincing that the newspaper reporter felt he should check once again with the Fair Elections Committee. Although James and Okey did not want to make the names public at this particular time and preferred to show them only to the Federal Bureau of Investigation, they reluctantly agreed to pick two names at random to prove their allegation. According to an official death certificate, Peter Maynard had died in November, 1960. The voting record showed that he was still registered and that he had voted in a special state and county election in 1963. According to the county records in 1966, Maynard voted again in the general election. Adam Woods had died in July, 1963, according to his death certificate. The official record showed that he had voted in the 1964 primary election and again in 1966 on a special bond levy. Woods was not challenged during the biennial checkup. West Virginia law required the office of the county clerk to conduct a check of the voter registration lists every two years, and all ineligible voters were to be removed from the lists. Had it not been for the Fair Elections Committee, Woods could have been voted again in the upcoming primary.

Chafin was asked about these two cases. He first claimed that someone had altered the registration cards to make it look as though Maynard and Woods had voted. But then he reluctantly stated, "There is a good possibility that someone did vote them." Chafin charged that members of the Fair Elections Committee "are just disgruntled people trying to further their own cause in the electoral process." He continued, "They didn't give us a chance. They started challenging before we could remove from the rolls the names that were not okayed by the registrars. If they had stayed away from us, we would have done a faster job and a better job."

When the same reporter interviewed T. I. Varney, a member of the House of Delegates from Mingo and the county probation officer, Varney accused the VISTA volunteers of being the instigators of the fair elections movement. He said, "They are dirty, nasty; they won't shave. As far as I'm concerned, the majority of them are communist inspired." Later, Varney said, "Those VISTA's—they are going to trip up before they leave here. That's no threat, but it's going to happen."

Of course, padded registrations were only one devious

145

means that the local political machine used to maintain its power. James Washington charged that in the county there were professional vote stealers who could mechanically manipulate the voting machines and actually prevent a machine from tallying a vote for the opposing candidate. He claimed the machines were rigged prior to election day.

Herbert Meade, a disabled coal miner from Marrowbone, a community located in the extreme western part of the county, described best how a precinct is stolen by the election officials when he addressed a group of Fair Elections Committee workers at a strategy meeting. As Meade explained it, the machines did not have to be mechanically rigged. "Now, you people all know how they operate the elections in each of the precincts. First of all, the three Democratic election officers and the two Republican election officers are usually in cahoots. So, actually, you have no one inside the house watching the election to make sure it is conducted in a fair manner. On the outside, working the grounds, they will have several of their stooges clearing the voters as they are hauled in. They give them a slate of the machine-picked candidates and tell them to see a certain election worker inside. Once they are inside the polling precinct, the election worker will take the card and go inside the voting machine with the individual and pull the levers for the machine candidates. Using a code of some sort, he will mark the card, give it back to the voter, and tell him to see a certain precinct worker on the outside. The voter is taken behind the building, put in a car, and paid—sometimes $5 or $10—for his vote. Welfare recipients are also intimidated and forced to vote the machine slate."

One citizen testified, "Before I was eighteen years old, I was registered to vote. The man who registered me—he is dead now—he was a part of this crooked politics. At that time, they gave Boone County whisky to go along. My dad was a coal miner for fifty years. I was born here in Mingo County. When it comes election time, they'll take you up to the house in a car." (All Mingo County residents referred to the polling precinct as a "house.") The man continued, "Last time I voted, they give me a little slip of paper saying how to vote. In the house, after you've sold your vote, they give you a green stamp to bring back to the man outside. They might pay around $5 to buy your vote. They'll give you $2 and put $3 in their pocket or maybe they'll give you $3 and a couple pints of whisky. Usually in a primary they'll pay more. That helps the local crooks. It's the local candidates they want to get elected. They don't care as much about the congressman or the governor. Most of the people around here, they don't know how to read and write, so they just take you in and vote you. I didn't even vote the last time. I just got tired of it. Those politicians, they herd you up there like cattle and promise you jobs, but during election time is the only time they'll talk to you. Sometimes they'll give a guy a job on the State Road and fire him after the election. But selling your vote to most people is a routine thing. They just herd you up there and say, 'Here's your money; here's your whisky.' If you don't want to go along after you once sold, you've got to watch every turn you make, lest someone will arrest you. I wrote a letter to Washington about it once, but I never did hear about it. My personal feeling is that what we have here is worse than communism ever could be."

To further educate the poor in matters concerning the political process, and especially the way elections were conducted in Mingo, a nonpartisan organization was estab-

147

lished, relying on the community action groups for its membership. It was named the Political Action League. The first task was to draft a political platform that incorporated all the issues that had become of concern to poor people, such as corrupt elections, unfair taxes, and inadequate education. Afterward, a committee was selected to seek out people who would be interested in becoming candidates and who could support the Political Action League platform. Within a short time, a full slate of candidates was selected and publicly endorsed. Arrangements to hold political rallies all over the county were being made in an effort to discuss the issues and to introduce the candidates. Decals and bumper stickers were printed and distributed throughout the county, along with literature explaining the Political Action League platform and giving biographical data on the candidates.

11

As the May primary election drew close, the activities of the Fair Elections Committee picked up momentum. Hundreds of people were being challenged as ineligible voters, and there was talk throughout the county that the FBI was already investigating the complaints made by the fair elections workers. The candidates endorsed by the Political Action League were attending rallies every night. The rallies usually included some gospel singing followed by a talk by one or two of the candidates. In many instances, the rallies reached the fervor of an old-time revival meeting.

For the first time in years, there were candidates challenging the Noah Floyd machine. Two of the three county commissioner positions were to be filled, seats vital to the survival of any political machine because the commissioners control county expenditures. But, within the county, the most heated race concerned the Board of Education. There were two seats to be filled, and six candidates were running, including two endorsed by the Political Action League and the Mingo County Education Committee, which was composed primarily of poor parents who were interested in obtaining free hot lunches for their children. Rumors in political circles were that Noah was making an attempt to elect two of his men to the Board of Education. If this was true, it would have been the first time in a decade that he had openly challenged the Board of Education. If successful, he would control all the elected offices in the county.

On March 15, in the late afternoon, I received a telephone call from Gladoula White. The news she related was what we had feared and anticipated for a long time. "Huey, I have just learned through my source at the courthouse that a letter has been sent to the OEO by the County Court requesting that they become the sponsor of the community action agency."

Her source was Mona Evans, a middle-aged woman who had been a friend of Gladoula's down through the years and who worked for Tom Chafin. She had managed to retrieve a copy of the letter from the wastebasket.

The following morning, I called Bob Curry in an effort to learn whether he had received the letter. He indicated that the letter would go to the regional director and he would never see a copy of it, and he suggested that we take any kind of action we felt necessary, adding that he would attempt to keep us informed if he learned any new information. The same evening, I called a special meeting of the community action group chairmen to talk above a course of action to prevent the take-over.

Everyone was disturbed by the news and puzzled about what to do. Herbert Meade, sitting looking down at the floor, with his head supported by both hands, said, "I have been expecting this. It seems, as soon as we get rid of one obstacle, another one pops up. First it was Gerald Chafin, and now it's Noah Floyd."

Everyone was looking to me for an answer. The only thing I could logically come up with was a protest demonstration in front of the courthouse. Yet, I was not sure how receptive the people would be to a demonstration. They had heard vaguely of riots and demonstrations in the cities, and most would probably associate a demonstration with a riot. Anyway, I cautiously approached them with the idea, and, when I had finished talking, Herb Meade rose from his chair and strongly supported my suggestion: "I believe Perry's right. It is our only way to fight back. I don't know if they will understand, but, just maybe, if we can get enough people out, it will make an impression on them. Besides, the primary election is just around the corner, and maybe we can scare them into retracting their decision."

The chairmen from the other groups all agreed. Oscar Dingess said, "I can get three hundred people out from Dingess. What we ought to do is go down and burn that damn courthouse to the ground."

"That's exactly what we ought to do," chimed in Lewis White. "Why, them no good sons of bitches want everything they can get their hands on, and they don't want to give us poor people nary a thing."

"They ain't nothing but a bunch of crooks; that's all they are," said Whitt Collins.

After an additional hour's discussion, it was agreed to hold the mass demonstration on March 30. Everyone was to work hard getting the people out and, above all, educating them as to what the County Court was attempting to do. It was also decided that a news release should be prepared regarding the County Court's decision, because the Court was making an effort to keep it a secret.

The next morning, we issued the following press release to the *Williamson Daily News*.

In a statement of intention directed to the Office of Economic Opportunity, Washington, D.C., the Mingo County Court has requested the abolishment of the EOC as the anti-poverty agency in Mingo County. The statement, signed by W. A. Myers, President, says the County Court wishes to either set up a new nonprofit organization or designate themselves as the poverty agency.

The article quoted what James Marcum had said at the Wednesday night meeting of the community action chairmen, which was "I can hardly wait until I get the chance to tell Washington about how sorry our County Court members are and what they would do with a program involving $1,200,000. Let the politicians know now they haven't seen a fight like they are going to see now." "Uncle Jim," as we all called him, was nearing seventy years of age and probably understood Mingo politics better than any of us.

James Washington was also quoted:

They had a chance to create a county housing authority which would have constructed low-income housing and would have been a hundred percent federally financed, and as it turned out, they would not even create the authority! Look at the economic development survey done by competent planners for the county at a cost of $48,000 to H.U.D. Why haven't they implemented it? What assistance have they given the small towns in developing sewage and water projects? Why haven't they hired a professional planner? While the people trod in mud and drink unsafe water, they sit in a million dollar courthouse, decorated with modern furniture and fine carpet paid for by the taxpayers, trying to figure out how they can win another election and continue to fool the people. Let them know now the people of Mingo will tolerate it no longer.

The following days were spent getting word out and coordinating the planned demonstration. It was a must that there be no violence. I invited Jeff Monroe from the State Office of Economic Opportunity to attend. Jeff was the only good thing in the Hulett Smith administration. Although he worked for the governor, he was always supporting the poor people's groups throughout the state.

The protest was planned for early Saturday morning, on the same day the trial for fair elections workers was scheduled to be held at 4:00 P.M. in Gilbert. I rode to Williamson with Larry Hamrick, the assistant director of the EOC, early that morning. On the way, we reflected upon what had been accomplished in the county during three years, even with all the resistance that had been put up by the establishment.

"You know, Larry, it is no wonder that the County Court, or should I say Noah Floyd, wants the poverty program. Here we have over a million dollars and about six hundred people on the payroll. If they are able to take it over, every one of those people will be fired, and they will give the jobs to their friends."

Larry replied, "There is no doubt about that. And I hate to think what they would do to the Head Start Program."

The Head Start Program was considered a model program by the OEO. It was directed by Leah Curry, a Mingo native in her mid-twenties. Leah was the daughter of an old-line politician who worked for the Board of Education, but she did not allow that alliance to stand in her way. She had been able to get the parents involved in the program, and she was using welfare mothers as teachers. This procedure was hard for the professional teachers and school administrators to swallow, but the women were doing a beautiful job. Three hundred and twenty-five five-year-old children were involved in the ten-month program. Mingo was one of two counties that had a full-year Head Start Program in the state. The others were held only during the summer months and under the auspices of the local boards of education.

I glanced at Larry. "I'm sure Leah will have all her Head Start parents and teachers out today. You know, that will make quite a crowd in itself."

As we drove down Pigeon Creek toward Williamson, we could see people standing along the road, waiting for their rides. "It sure looks good," I commented to Larry.

When we arrived in Williamson at 9:30, the streets were crowded. Lawrence Phelps had already parked his car in front of the courthouse. It was equipped with a public address system with two large speakers facing in opposite directions.

We parked in the city parking lot and walked toward the courthouse, meeting Oscar Dingess coming toward us.

"Hey, do you know that Governor Smith has sent thirteen carloads of state police in here today?"

"No. But, come to think of it, we did see two carloads pass through Gilbert just as we were leaving."

"What's he think, that we'll burn the courthouse down?"

By 10:00, more than two thousand people had gathered in front of the courthouse chanting and yelling, "No!" to the County Court's bid to take over their program. Signs were waving, and Brooks Lawson, Sr., opened the window of his second-story office in the First National Bank building to observe the demonstration. Brooks was considered the most sophisticated of the several county lawyers that practiced in Williamson. He had long dabbled in politics, but, being a Republican, he was never able to win any of the offices he ran for. The expression on his face showed that he was delighted—not because he believed in the poor but because he was in favor of any type of opposition leveled against Democrats.

At 10:30, Jeff Monroe arrived with K. W. Lee, a reporter from the *Charleston Gazette*. K. W. had been following the activities of the Fair Elections Committee and was very much excited about the movement in Mingo. During World War II, he had been a pilot in the Japanese Air Force, and he had since become a U.S. citizen. Although I had never met him, I had worked with him by telephone because I had coordinated most of the publicity for the Fair Elections Committee.

K. W. was smiling broadly as he came past me up the street to snap pictures of the event. "My God, Perry, what have you got going on here?"

Jeff said, as he reached to shake hands, "I brought that 'Jap' pilot with me; figured you would need as much publicity as you could get. It's going to be a tough battle."

"Where does Smith stand on this matter?" I asked.

Jeff replied, "To tell you the truth, I don't know. You know he is a politician, and they are unpredictable."

"You are right, Jeff. There is no question that Noah, being a veteran member of the state Senate can put a considerable amount of pressure on the governor. I am surprised he allowed you to come down here."

"He doesn't always know where I am and what I am doing." Jeff smiled. "I'll tell you one thing, Perry; if the rest of West Virginia's poor were organized the way you are here in Mingo, the governor would be listening to the poor rather than Noah."

As we rounded the corner, walking toward the courthouse, Nimrod Workman, a disabled coal miner, had taken over the public address system and was criticizing the county commissioners for their attempt to take over the agency: "You politicians are no better than the United Mine Workers. I worked in the mines for forty years, and that Union has denied me everything—my welfare pension, my hospital card—and now you politicians are wanting to deny us of our program." Nimrod sounded more like a hellfire-and-damnation Baptist preacher than a poverty crusader. Perhaps this was the reason he was always effective in getting his messages across.

Several deputy sheriffs were guarding the entrance of the courthouse. The state police were nowhere in sight. Occasionally, T. I. Varney would peep through a window and stare at the crowd. Arthur White, a young man in his late twenties, standing next to a deputy sheriff on the courthouse steps, yelled, "Huey Perry is a no-good son of a bitch!" Rossi Bucci, a city policeman, quieted him, but the deputy made no attempt to calm him. Arthur worked for the State Road Commission.

A delegation of five, headed by Herb Meade, went in and invited the three county commissioners outside to answer questions. Meanwhile, one demonstrator after the other was taking turns speaking over the public address system.

Lawrence Phelps, with a fairly large chew of tobacco pushing out his left cheek, leaned forward on his toes and shouted over the crowd, "Shorty, can you hear me?" He was making reference to Shorty Myers, who was president of the commissioners. Shorty, who stood six feet five inches tall, had been elected in 1936 and consecutively thereafter. He was in his eighties and more than likely did not even know what was going on outside.

Phelps continued, "Shorty, you are still a servant of the

people. In old England, if a king didn't like you, he would cut your head off. Now, if they don't like you, they'll cut off your project!"

There was laughter and wild applause from the crowd.

At that point, several of the poor people recognized Jeff and insisted that he speak. It was the shortest speech of the day.

"No poverty program should ever be administered by a county court if it is to be effective," Jeff said, and he promised that he would do everything in his power to prevent the commissioners from taking over the poverty agency.

Herb Meade then took the microphone to report to the people the negative reaction of the commissioners, who would not come outside, and concluded the demonstration, which had lasted one hour, by saying, "You people know what has to be done; now, let's go back to our homes in the hollers and get on with the job."

Again there was loud applause, and the crowd began to disperse. Many of them were driving to Gilbert to witness the trial of the fair elections workers.

12

At 4:00 P.M. on March 30, the courtroom
of Magistrate Arden Mounts was jammed with spectators
who had gathered to witness the trial of the fair elections
workers. About half the crowd were ardent supporters of
the county political machine.

Mounts had been justice of the peace in Stafford District
for more than twenty years. His offices and courtroom were
located on the second floor of a building that also housed
a garage he owned. In his younger days he had been a
motorcycle enthusiast and had lost his left leg when his
cycle collided head-on with a log truck about two miles
from his birthplace on Gilbert Creek. He now walked with
the aid of an artificial limb.

Mounts's nephew Roger was standing at the base of the
steps leading to the courtroom as we entered. "Hey, come
on up and watch the fun," he called to a friend. "Arden is
going to sock it to them fair election workers today."

"I hope he gives them a year," said the friend. "All they
are is a bunch of troublemakers."

More than a hundred fair elections workers had gathered

outside the garage and were milling around, awaiting the trial. The defendants were Judy Trent, Alma Jean Justice, and Hayes Hatfield. Cleo Jones, the Fair Elections Committee's attorney, had arrived from Charleston at about 3:30 and had consulted with the three arrested workers and also with James Washington. The committee had first approached Jones because he had attempted to bring about an investigation of the AFDCU program in Mingo County immediately after the EOC public hearing in February, 1967, in which Floyd had been exposed. Jones, a soft-spoken man, always smoked a pipe.

Although the Justice of the Peace Court had no jurisdiction in cases dealing with elections, everyone felt certain that Mounts would ignore the law and go ahead with the trial. Mounts was one of the last people to enter the courtroom. He walked straight to his desk, turned and looked toward the crowd, and said, "This court is now in order." He proceeded: "I have several warrants here—one for Mrs. Judy Trent, which was sworn out by Frank Fortener. This is Mr. Fortener over here." Mounts pointed to his left.

Fortener was sitting facing the crowd. A coal miner in his early fifties, he had also been involved in local politics. He had run unsuccessfully for justice of the peace on several occasions but had always been a staunch supporter of the Democratic machine. Judy Trent had challenged his right to be registered, on the grounds that he lived outside the precinct, which, according to West Virginia election law, was a legal challenge.

Mounts continued, "Now everyone here knows that Frank Fortener has been a legal voter of this district for years and years, and it is unfortunate that this here man's right to vote has been challenged."

Jones rose to his feet and asked Mounts, "Are you proceeding with the trial of Mrs. Trent?"

Mounts replied, "Yeah. And just who are you?"

"My name is Cleo Jones. I am an attorney, and I reside in the city of Charleston. I am here to represent my client, Mrs. Judy Trent."

Mounts hesitated and fumbled through the West Virginia Code, which was lying open on his desk. Sitting down for the first time in his chair, he said, "Would Judy Trent step forward and be sworn in?"

Mrs. Trent took a seat beside Mounts's desk.

"Would you hold your right hand up, Mrs. Trent? Do you swear to tell the truth, the whole truth, and nothing else, so help you God?" Mounts asked.

Mrs. Trent replied, "I do."

Mounts, looking over at Fortener, asked, "Mr. Fortener, do you have an attorney to represent you?"

"No," said Fortener.

Mounts proceeded with the preliminary instructions, and Attorney Jones asked Mounts to read the warrant and the charges against Mrs. Trent.

"Mr. Jones," Mounts replied, "I just told you what she was charged with, but, if it'll satisfy you, I'll read the warrant."

The warrant was identical in wording to all the rest, with the exception of the one served on Hayes Hatfield. In his haste to issue a warrant against Hatfield, the justice of the peace had charged him with challenging his own right to vote. The warrant against him had been sworn out by Carl Mounts, who was the father of Arden Mounts.

Mounts, looking at Mrs. Trent, asked, "How do you plead?"

She replied, "Innocent."

Mounts continued, "Did you or did you not challenge Mr. Frank Fortener's right to vote?"

Mrs. Trent replied, "No, I did not challenge his right to vote; I challenged his right to be registered, because he was voting in the wrong precinct."

"Now, if you challenge a person's right to be registered, you're actually challenging his right to vote," said Mounts.

At this point, Jones interrupted: "Mr. Mounts, I would like to inform you that you, as a justice of the peace, under the West Virginia statute, do not have the authority to try an election case."

Turning very red in the face, Mounts shouted, "I'll have you know, Mr. Jones, I am the damned judge here in this court, and there ain't no two-bit lawyer gonna come in here from Charleston and tell me how I've gotta conduct my court. And I want you to know one damned thing right now: I've been up against a helluva lot better attorneys than you. Because you're from Charleston is no sign you think you're gonna come in here and scare me to death."

"I'm not attempting to scare you to death." Jones did not raise his voice.

Again Mounts shouted, "I'm the judge here!"

Again Jones proceeded to explain that, under the law, justices of the peace were not qualified to do anything in election matters other than dismiss charges or hold the accused for a grand jury hearing.

Mounts slammed shut the West Virginia Code Book on his desk. "It's a misdemeanor, and I have the right to try it, and that is that!" He then turned to Mrs. Trent. "You're going to have to prove your innocence, or I'm going to have to find you guilty."

"It is up to the man making the charges to prove she is guilty," Jones protested.

"The defendant has to prove it. She certainly has to prove it in my court!" The angry justice of the peace turned back to Mrs. Trent. "Can you prove your innocence?"

Mrs. Trent replied, "I do not think that I am guilty of anything. I only challenged the man's right to be registered because he was voting outside the precinct in which he lives."

Mounts replied, "In that case, I don't have any further questions."

Jones rose to his feet. However, before he could utter a sound, Mounts yelled, "One more wise crack out of you, Jones, and I'm gonna fine you for contempt of court!"

Without hesitating, Mounts then called for Fortener to take the seat beside the desk, which was used as the witness's chair. "Mr. Fortener, will you raise your right hand? Do you swear to tell the truth, the whole truth, and nothing but the truth, so help you God?"

Mr. Fortener replied, "I do." He appeared to be quite nervous as he faced the crowd.

Mounts asked, "What is your name?"

"My name is Frank Fortener, and I live up on Gilbert Creek."

Mounts continued, "Mr. Fortener, you have charged a Judy Trent with challenging your right to vote. Is that right?"

"Yes."

Mounts looked at the crowd as if he had scored a major point and said, "No more questions." He looked toward Jones. "Now, Mr. Jones, if you can follow the procedure that we use here in this court, you may question the plaintiff."

Jones proceeded with his questioning by asking the plaintiff his name and where he resided. Once again, Fortener explained that he resided at Gilbert Creek.

Jones asked, "Mr. Fortener, what is the precinct number at Gilbert Creek?"

Fortener replied, "I think it is number 73."

"Do you vote at number 73?" Jones asked.

Fortener replied, "No, I vote at number 75, the city hall precinct in the city of Gilbert."

Jones continued, "Do you live in the town of Gilbert?"

Fortener answered, "No, I explained to you a minute ago that I live at Gilbert Creek."

"Then, why do you not vote at Gilbert Creek?"

Fortener replied, "I've always voted at Gilbert, as long as I can remember."

Jones countered, "Then you live in one precinct and vote in another. Is that true?"

Fortener replied, "Yes."

Mounts interrupted: "I don't give a Goddamn where he lives. The man votes in Stafford District, and he's voted there all of his life, and I don't see why this damned bunch of Fair Elections Committee people has got any right to tell a man where he can vote and where he can't vote."

Sensing the hopelessness of the situation, Jones now told Mounts that he had no more questions.

"Will the defendant rise?" Mounts asked.

Mrs. Trent stood slowly.

"Mrs. Trent, I'm going to find you guilty of challenging this man's right to vote, and I'm gonna give you the maximum sentence. I'm gonna fine you $100 and give you sixty days in jail."

Jones immediately informed Mounts that the case would be appealed to the Circuit Court.

Mounts said, "I don't give a damn if you appeal it to the Supreme Court. I find her guilty here in this court at least, anyway."

Mounts jotted a few notes down on a legal pad and then proceeded to pull the second warrant from his files. "Now, this case was not scheduled for today, but we have both the defendant and the plaintiff here, and, if it's all right with them, we'll proceed with the second trial."

Hayes Hatfield, who was one of the youngest members of the Fair Elections Committee, had taken a very active part since his return to the county. He had been working in Ohio. Mounts's father, Carl, lived in another district, and, according to West Virginia election law, it was illegal to be registered in one district and live in another. The voting records indicated that Carl Mounts had voted at Cline, which was precinct number 73, for the last forty years. However, Mounts had moved to another district and had continued to vote in the Stafford District, and he had been challenged by Hatfield on these grounds.

Hayes had been the first to notice that the warrant served on him was faulty, actually charging him with challenging his own right to be registered. As soon as Hayes had been sworn in, attorney Jones informed Mounts that the warrant was faulty and asked that the case be dismissed on those grounds. Mounts once again read the warrant, and he admitted that it was faulty. He promptly pulled from his desk a clean warrant and proceeded to write it up on the spot. Then he asked his father to step forward and sign it. "Now we've got a warrant that'll stand up in court," he said. "However, since this warrant involves my father, I think that I should not try the case; so I'm going to step aside."

Another justice of the peace from the same district was standing in the back of the courtroom. Mounts asked him to conduct the trial. The other justice of the peace refused to do so, whereupon Mounts dismissed the case against Hatfield.

The plaintiff against Mrs. Alma Jean Justice did not appear, and so the third case was also dismissed.

Over the next two weeks, other fair elections workers were arrested and additional justice-of-the-peace trials were conducted in three different courts throughout the county. All followed a pattern. The warrants were identical, and the justices of the peace interpreted the law in the same manner. Clearly, an attempt by the political machine to frighten the Fair Elections Committee workers was under way. Jones assured James Washington and his people that they should continue purging the names. He said he would always be available to represent them, without any fee.

A strategy meeting was called by the Fair Elections Committee. It was evident that there had been violation of the civil rights of the fair elections workers who had been arrested and convicted. It was also evident that no justice would be rendered in Mingo County. I attended the strategy meeting and suggested to the group that perhaps it should charter a bus and take its case directly to the Department of Justice in Washington, D.C. Cleo Jones, the attorney, also recommended the strategy, and enthusiasm for the idea was great.

The following Monday, I called the Department of Justice and requested an appointment for the group. I talked with Steven Pollock, who was in the election fraud and civil rights division of the Department, and explained to him what had been taking place in Mingo County. He listened very intently and asked several questions. He appeared to be receptive to the idea of the appointment until I explained to him that an entire busload of poor people wanted to present their case directly to him. He could not understand why it was necessary for the entire busload to come to Washington, and he suggested that maybe two or three representatives from the delegation could handle the situation better. I explained to him that this was a group of poor people who were interested in democracy for their county and that to send only two or three would destroy the effectiveness of the group. "We have never had a situation where an entire busload of people have asked for an appointment before," he finally said. "I will have to take this matter up with the higher officials and call you back later this afternoon."

When he called back, he was still insisting that a small delegation rather than the large group come to Washington. At this point, I asked him to speak with Claudia Schecter, an Appalachian Volunteer who had been working very closely with the Fair Elections Committee and who was standing by on an extension. Claudia attempted to explain why it was important for the larger group to attend the meeting rather than a small delegation. She told Pollock that the group had information it wanted to give to the Department of Justice and wanted to give it in person. She said that she believed there was a conspiracy by the county politicians to halt the challenging of the illegally registered voters within the county. Pollock was sympathetic but still did not agree to see the entire delegation. However, at Claudia's insistence, he promised to call us up again the next day with some additional information.

When Pollock called the following morning, he asked for Claudia. After she had been on the phone with him for more than twenty minutes, she came to my office and said, "I wish you would talk with that son of a gun with the Department of Justice; he just doesn't understand what the situation is." Once more I gave Pollock my arguments as to why it was necessary for the entire group to come, and once more he gave me his arguments that it was the policy of the Department of Justice for a complaint to be filed and that the complaint could be filed by a small group as easily as a large group. At this point, I said that, regardless of whether they would have an appointment or not, at least forty members of the Fair Elections Committee would be in Washington in two days, and I asked that he make every effort to talk with them. Later in the day, he called again and said that he had talked with other people in the Department of Justice. They had reached the decision that they would see the entire delegation.

Money was raised locally, and a bus was chartered. It was decided that Claudia Schecter and Larry Hamrick would make the trip with the delegation and handle all arrangements. Altogether, thirty-six Mingo County people active in the Fair Elections Committee and community action groups attended the Washington meeting. Seven members of the group spent six hours with the Federal Bureau of Investigation, giving statements of their knowledge of violations in the registration rolls of the county. The group also met with Robert Rosthall, chief of the election fraud division of the Justice Department; Edgar Brown, representing the criminal division; and Gary J. Greenberg, representing the civil rights division. The FBI officials informed the

167

group that the statements made individually would be screened and sent to FBI headquarters and to the Justice Department, which would then set a course of action.

While they were in Washington, members of the Mingo County delegation also met with Congressman Jim Kee and Senators Jennings Randolph and Robert C. Byrd. Several of the group walked out during the meeting with Byrd because of his negative attitude toward them. Senator Randolph met with the entire group and listened sympathetically to its account of the problems encountered by the Fair Elections Committee, as well as those caused by the Green Amendment making possible a County Court takeover of the antipoverty agency. After the meeting, Alma Jean Justice discovered that she had challenged four sisters of one of Senator Randolph's assistants. Mrs. Justice said the assistant was very much surprised because all the sisters had left the county before they reached voting age.

Immediately after the group returned to Mingo County, enthusiastic because of the response it had received in Washington, it made plans to go to Charleston to seek state assistance with its clean elections drive. James Washington announced that a delegation of ten members would meet with the West Virginia secretary of state, Robert D. Bailey, the following week to demand a prompt investigation of alleged electoral fraud in the county. At this meeting Alma Jean Justice explained how elections were stolen.

Pointing to the Wharncliffe precinct in Stafford District, which had been cited as one with flagrant abuses of the election laws and padded registration, she said, "When I first challenged Wharncliffe, I found 511 names on the book. Everyone had voted, or been voted, in 1966, but there were only about 200 people who lived there. Two days later I went back to check if the people I had challenged had been removed. Only a few had been removed, and now there were 600 on the books—with a stack of cards yet to go in."

Apparently disturbed by the Fair Elections Committee's activities, especially after the Washington and Charleston trips, Tom Chafin issued a statement to the *Williamson Daily News:*

> During my six years as Mingo County Court Clerk, I and my staff have extended to every visitor to my office courtesy and respect. Never have I threatened any citizens, Fair Elections Committee or otherwise, with disrespect or intimidation. The Fair Elections Committee has tried time and time again to lead people to believe that my office and other courthouse employees have intimidated Fair Elections Committee workers. Nothing could be farther from the truth.
>
> During the past several months, hundreds of visitors have come to my office. I have treated each of them with the respect and dignity I would expect should I visit their office or home. Although false charges have been made against me, my office staff, and other elected officials, I insisted that the same people making these false charges be treated with the utmost respect when they visited my office.
>
> We are here in the courthouse at the wishes of the people of Mingo County. The Fair Elections Committee did not elect me, nor will they defeat me. Only the people of Mingo County whom I have served honestly and faithfully can defeat me.

On May 1, in an effort to apply additional pressure to the Noah Floyd machine, nine community action chairmen filed a court suit asking the removal from office of five county officials. The ouster petition accused W. R. Myers, Sr., Harry Artis, and C. J. "Ben" Hamilton—all County Court commissioners—Sheriff Steve Adkins, and County

Clerk Tom Chafin of official misconduct, malfeasance in office, incompetence, neglect of duty, and gross immorality.

Specifically, the suit accused the County Court of fraudulently seeking U.S. Civil Defense funds for radio equipment for use by the sheriff's department and Civil Defense Unit. The petitioners alleged that the County Court sought the money on a matching basis, although there was no such fund in the county budget, and that radio equipment had already been purchased and was in use by the sheriff's department. The sheriff, in turn, was accused of illegally obtaining a $31,500 loan from the Matewan National Bank for the entire amount of the equipment. The suit alleged that Sheriff Adkins had required Lester LaPrade, who sold and installed the equipment, to pay a $1,000 kickback as part of the conditions for furnishing the radio equipment. Adkins later supposedly raised the kickback to $1,500, saying that the additional $500 was to go to the new court member, Harry Artis.

Other charges accused Adkins, in concert with the court members, of directing LaPrade to prepare bids in such a way that no competitors could bid for the radio equipment and of falsifying the application for the civil defense radio fund. Allegations involving the County Court clerk and the court were related to the activities of the Fair Elections Committee. The clerk and the court were charged with refusing to open public records to interested voters, despite the latter's request, and purposely impeding all efforts to purge the county registration rolls of unqualified voters.

More than a month's research had gone into the preparation of this suit. Although LaPrade had agreed to turn state's evidence, we believed that the suit would eventually be thrown out because it had to be tried in Mingo County, and the judge, Charles Ferguson, was a close friend of all the defendants. Some people considered it the same as if the defendants were trying themselves. Nevertheless, the newspaper publicity that accompanied the filing of the suit produced a negative feeling toward Mingo's elected officials. People were saying, "They're probably guilty, but nothing will ever come of it." By filing the petition after the mass demonstration, we hoped to have some effect upon the decision as to who would operate the poverty agency.

There was no doubt now that the political machine was shaken. The demonstration, followed by the Fair Elections activities and the ensuing justice-of-the-peace trials, the trip to Washington, and the investigation by the Justice Department into civil rights violations, was beginning to have an effect, not only in Mingo but in the entire state. The rumor in Charleston was that many other political bosses in the southern counties were worried about Mingo's antipoverty activities and feared that the movement would spread to their counties. Already, the county courts of Webster, Raleigh, Cabell, Wayne, and Lincoln counties were making efforts to take over the community action programs in their counties. According to Jeff Monroe, Noah was constantly prodding Governor Smith to do something about Mingo's antipoverty program. Noah had also told Jeff that, if something was not done soon, there would not be a Democratic Party left in Mingo.

But, if Noah was feeling pressed, he also evidently had concluded that he had reached the apex of his power, and he began quietly to support two candidates of his own for the Board of Education against the incumbent board. This move was surprising, for in the past there had always been an alliance between Noah and the Board of Education. Perhaps he thought that the two candidates who were endorsed by the Political Action League would pull votes from the incumbents, thus allowing him to slip his two candidates in.

Noah's decision to support two of his own candidates raised a very serious question within the poverty agency. If the Political Action League candidates did pull several hundred votes from the incumbent board, it was almost certain that Noah's candidates would win. With control of the school board, it would be much easier for him to take over the EOC. I began immediately to discuss this possibility with the community action leaders and even with the candidates the Political Action League was sponsoring. It was agreed that a decision on whether our support would secretly go to the incumbents rather than to the Political Action League candidates would be withheld until the very last. The League candidates agreed wholeheartedly with this strategy, even if it might mean they would lose support. The possibility of completely dividing Noah and the board could, it was felt, perhaps be the first step in the eventual destruction of Noah's power.

As the primary neared, a flow of absentee voting began. In West Virginia, absentee voting opens thirty days before an election, and all an absentee voter has to do in order to cast his ballot is to declare that he will be out of the county on election day. In 1964, over three thousand voters had declared that they would be out of the county on election day and, as a result, a third of Mingo's voters had already cast their votes before the election, with more than 90 per cent of the ballots marked the same way. The state legislators who went to Charleston had made it easy for political bosses to steal elections in this manner. Absentee voting was prevalent in all the coal counties in the state. Throughout the month of May, Ike Newsome and other employees of the county and state devoted most of their time to bringing people into the courthouse from outlying areas of the county to vote absentee ballots. Although the Fair Elections Committee posted observers in the Circuit Court clerk's office, where absentee voting took place, at best the observers prevented only a few from voting.

Young Jay Rockefeller, a Democratic candidate for secretary of state, was invited by the Fair Elections Committee to observe the absentee voting in Mingo. Afterward, he pledged his fullest support of, and cooperation with, the work of the committee, adding that he had personally observed the voting of an absurd number of absentee ballots in full view of officials, rather than in private as the law required, and had noted also the transportation of absentee voters to the courthouse in state-owned cars. Rockefeller, who had come to West Virginia as a poverty worker and been almost instantly elected to the state House of Delegates, was running against two old-line politicians, neither of whom presented much of a challenge. His presence in the state had already created much confusion in the Democratic organization and the establishment, which found it difficult to understand why a long-haired VISTA-worker Rockefeller, possessing an abundance of wealth, would suddenly appear on the West Virginia political scene. Even more confusing to Noah was the fact that Jay now came to Mingo and met with poor people and me, rather than with Noah and his friends. Jay became a strong ally of the poverty agency and of the Fair Elections Committee and cooperated with us in our efforts to expose the corruption that was Mingo's legacy.

Being fully aware that the polling officials of the Democratic Party were all selected by Noah's machine, we made a plea to the Department of Justice and the President of the United States to send in federal poll observers for the election. The request was denied. There was much support, however, for using volunteer poll observers from VISTA, the Appalachian Volunteers, and young campaign workers for Senators Eugene McCarthy and Robert Kennedy. On election day, we had scores of volunteers observing the polls, taking notes, and obtaining affidavits documenting election fraud. But, even with all the poll watchers, the election was as corrupt as always.

Many of the poll watchers were abused by supporters of the machine. One incident involved Alma Jean Justice, who had been observing the polls at Wharncliffe precinct. She reported, "Constable Bob Owens tried everything to get me away from poll watching, including egging a group of young men to rape me." She said that the officer called her names, the mildest of which was "hussy." At one point, she said, he turned from her to the young men standing nearby and asked them, "Boys, which one of you wants to be first?"

A deputy sheriff struck another poll watcher inside the courthouse while the poll watcher was taking pictures of candidates mingling with voters standing in line. Still another poll watcher's camera was snatched away from him by a constable and thrown to the ground.

Lerly Murphy, an active Fair Elections Committee worker, said that her husband also tried to photograph activities outside a polling place. A deputy sheriff, she said, "told him if he took a picture he would shoot the camera out of his hands." She said her husband kept taking pictures, and the deputy tried to grab the camera away from him. "He stood his ground, and the officer didn't shoot."

All the information collected by poll observers was turned over to the Department of Justice and to the West Virginia Secretary of State. Both promised a thorough investigation.

Noah's candidates won all the races except those for the Board of Education—in which, at the last minute, the community action chairmen gave their support to the incumbent board members, which enabled them to win, although by fewer than three hundred votes. However, many observers felt this election had been a time of crucial mistakes for Noah. He had alienated a large number of people who were affiliated with the school system, and, above all, the *Williamson Daily News*, which in the past had always remained neutral when it came to his activities, but in this period ran several editorials praising the Fair Elections Committee and opposing Floyd. Also, and most important to us, there was now the possibility that the Board of Education would support the EOC in maintaining the antipoverty agency, rather than see Noah's forces in control of it—not because the Board supported the activities of the poverty agency but out of the necessity to weaken Noah.

An interesting footnote to the election was that Jay Rockefeller lost in Mingo. It was the only county in the state that gave him a negative vote. Sometime later he said, "I would have been terribly disappointed had I won the election in Mingo. It is the only county where you can get a fewer number of votes than your opposition and feel you have won."

13

After the primary, the County Court intensified its efforts to replace the EOC as the antipoverty agency. Soon, deputy sheriffs, constables, and state and county employees were going through every community and up every hollow and creek, getting people to sign a petition endorsing the take-over of the antipoverty agency by the County Court. In many instances, people signed, believing it would mean a new road, a new gymnasium, a lunchroom for their school, and in some cases even jobs for the people. The petition carriers managed to get signatures from other counties and even other states.

Hundreds of people later became angered when they learned what they had signed, but the devious effort of the County Court resulted in a petition containing more than eight thousand names. The EOC countered the petition by submitting to the OEO in Washington affidavits explaining that people were being deceived into signing.

In early June, I visited the OEO regional office to talk with Les Minkus, the legal counsel for the region, and Ed Cogen. "Is there anything at all we can do to save the agency?" I asked them.

Minkus looked at Cogen, and Cogen looked at Minkus. Each was waiting for the other to answer. Finally, Minkus began explaining the OEO policy.

"To be frank with you, Perry, we see very little hope. The final decision will naturally be made by the director of OEO in headquarters, and not by any of us in the regional office."

"Does that mean we are finished in Mingo?"

"Well, not exactly, although I don't see much hope, I don't think you should roll over and play dead. You know, the County Court must hold a public hearing before July 1. This would be a good place for the community people to voice their opposition."

Cogen interrupted: "Perry, we would like to go with you, but you know what our biggest problem is, pressure from the Congress, and especially Edith Green. In fact, she has been making a daily inquiry as to the progress of her amendment. And your own delegation from West Virginia —certainly Kee and Byrd would both like to see the County Court with the agency."

Why talk about Kee and Byrd? I thought. Everyone knows where they stand.

After thirty minutes of such talk, I mentioned that Jerry Chafin had been appointed by the County Court to transact all business between the court and the OEO regarding the planned take-over. Both Minkus and Cogen grinned. Cogen opened his top desk drawer and handed me a copy of the letter he had received designating Chafin as the court's official representative.

Minkus said, "There is one thing about Gerald Chafin. He is the most persistent fellow I have seen. He just doesn't give up."

"This move by the court has infuriated the community action people," I said. "Those few who were neutral when he was ousted are certain now it was a good move." I continued, "I hear he was up here last week."

Again Minkus and Cogen glanced at each other as if they were surprised that I knew Chafin had been there. Little did they realize that, in a rural county, as the Mingo saying goes, everybody "knows what you have done two days before you do it."

Cogen finally answered. "Yes, he and a friend were here. We spent about an hour with him and explained to him the time schedule that has been established to transfer the community action agencies. Incidentally, the date is February 1, 1969. He had been in a meeting with Frank Tsutras and Jim Kee before he came over here. You can figure that out for yourself."

No mention of Chafin's visit would have been made if I had not brought the subject up myself, I was convinced. At this point in the meeting, I was also convinced that we could expect no help from the OEO. As usual, everyone with a grade level of G.S. 15 or above was running scared for his job as a result of pressure from some congressman.

"There is a provision in the Green Amendment stating in general terms that the state and federal law must not conflict if a state has a law governing the establishment of antipoverty agencies," I told Minkus. "In West Virginia there is a state law that prevents a county court from delegating responsibility to other people, which would be in conflict with OEO's requirement that all poverty agency boards be made up of one-third poor representatives. And the governor of the state is the only one who has the power to recognize a poverty agency."

"Yes," he replied, "we are aware of the West Virginia law. In fact, we have asked Jeff Monroe to get an interpretation from the West Virginia attorney general."

"If this would prevent the politicians from taking us over, I am sure, once they find it out, they will call a special session of the legislature."

Minkus answered, "Well, perhaps they will not be that smart."

As I walked down the long hall leading to the elevator, I thought that the meeting had been almost useless. If I were to tell the people in Mingo about the attitude of OEO officials regarding the take-over by the County Court, it would be the end. The politics of a federal bureaucracy was far too complicated for them to understand. Besides, the community action people had contact only with the field representatives, and almost all of them were young liberals who advocated more power to the people. The image the poor people had of the OEO and what I knew of agency attitudes were entirely different. If the EOC was to be saved, I knew that we would have to save it from our end. Somehow, I thought, I had to continue to give everybody hope and encouragement.

On June 11, the County Court published in the *Williamson Daily News* the following statement:

> Notice is hereby given that a public hearing has been set by the County Court of Mingo County, West Virginia, for the purpose of the general public, as well as any interested organization, expressing views on the question of the Court designating a community action agency for said Mingo County, West Virginia, as provided under the 1967 amendments to the Economic Opportunity Act. Said public hearing will be held June 22, 1968, one-thirty o'clock, p.m. D.S.T. at the Courthouse.

Originally, our strategy was to boycott the hearing. The court had already decided to become the antipoverty agency, and the hearing would be only a formality to fulfill OEO requirements. However, after giving the matter more careful consideration, we decided to voice strong opposition, mainly for the effect it might have on public opinion. Besides, absence of opposition at a public hearing would only strengthen the position of the County Court when the OEO made its decision.

The courtroom was packed on June 22. The community action people arrived at noon and immediately took up all the seats and most of the available standing room. At 1:15, Ben Hamilton, apointed president *pro tempore* in the absence of Shorty Myers, who was on vacation, arrived with the other commissioner, Harry Artis. Most of the other county politicians were present. T. I. Varney and Noah Floyd made a brief entrance, looked over the crowd, and left. Several deputy sheriffs stood nervously at each entrance.

Hamilton sat in the judge's chair, next to the witness stand. "Ladies and gentlemen," he began, "I want to emphasize that we do not have smoking in the courtroom. If you want to smoke, please step outside in the hall. The meeting will now come to order."

He spent the next few minutes reading the notice that had appeared in the paper and stating the rules established for the hearing. At one point, he said, "Now, in conformity with the requirements under Section 210(e) of the Act as amended for the establishment of community action agencies, the County Court has taken the necessary steps to designate itself as the community action agency, part of which is to give interested organizations and persons the opportunity to express their views before designation."

There was laughter from the crowd, and he pounded his gavel for order. He continued, "I would like to say here and now that the Mingo County Court has not engaged in a 'smear project' as we were accused in a news release. Quite the contrary, we have said very little regarding this, and the 'smear' tactics have been carried out by those opposing the County Court taking over the administration of the poverty program."

Again there was laughter from the crowd, and he rapped his gavel for order and glanced around toward a group of deputy sheriffs standing to his left.

"A time limit of one hour will be allotted for those who wish the County Court to take over the administration of the poverty program, and a time limit of one hour shall be allotted for those who wish the existing community action agency to continue to administer the program."

Floyd and T. I. Varney came back into the courtroom and took seats to the right of Hamilton, facing the crowd. I was sitting in the rear of the room, with several other EOC staff people.

"Now, those speaking for the County Court will start now, with Mr. Jerry Chafin addressing you at this time."

This was the first time I had seen Chafin since he had been ousted. Smiling, he stepped forward, carrying an armload of papers, and began: "Mr. Chairman, ladies and gentlemen, I am glad for this opportunity to appear before the County Court to state my views regarding the take-over of the EOC or the poverty program for administration by the County Court. Contrary to the gossip and the propaganda that has been spread out over the county by different officials of the EOC, the Green Amendment is quite clear.

The timetable has been set forth in the guidelines by the OEO in conformity with the Green Amendment, and the deadline or target date has been set for February 1, 1969."

Making that point, Chafin glanced up from his paper and hesitated before beginning again. "For some time, the Mingo County Economic Opportunity Commission was considered a model for the many programs that were administered by the OEO through the different community action groups. For some time in Mingo County, the Economic Opportunity Commission dealt with the programs that were set forth and approved by the OEO in Washington, but last summer, due to an insistence of the Appalachian Volunteers and VISTA's, they got into issues and politics. Where the state agencies had been receiving committees and sitting down with people to iron out problems, difficulties, changes that the people thought were needed, they immediately became uncooperative. They wouldn't meet with them. So they defeated the very purpose for which the Economic Opportunity Commission was designated and organized, and that was to mobilize all of the resources of Mingo County in helping to eliminate poverty. What they succeeded in doing was mobilizing the poor people. They forgot that it took the taxpayers' money and the cooperation of the state and federal agencies to complement these programs, to make these programs necessary."

There was no reaction from the audience as Chafin continued with his speech: "The EOC Board of Directors was made up at one time by approximately half of businessmen, but, through pressure, through tactics, under cover, these businessmen quit attending the meetings, quit taking part, because they said, 'I don't want any part of it.' Rather than to go into specific instances which have happened throughout this county, I would like to read a portion of an investigation or inspection of the Mingo County Economic Opportunity Commission that was held in March of this year. This investigation team was from Washington. It was a team from the Office of Economic Opportunity."

Chafin was now reading excerpts from an OEO evaluation report—for effect labeling it an "investigation." All the EOC board members had received copies and were well aware of its contents. Appearing extremely confident that he would soon have his old job back as president of the EOC, he waded through the bureaucratese as distinctly as his mountain accent would allow, occasionally breaking the reading with his own comments.

"Under 'Perceived Objectives'—this is what the EOC thinks they should be doing—'The over-all perceived objective of the EOC is to develop among the poor people in Mingo County democratic community organizations which are a tool for effecting institutional and political change in the county. The perceived objectives include the mobilization of human resources among the poor, the development of autonomous and independent leadership among the poor, and a deliberate, selective use of OEO-funded programs as a subtool for the achievement of the goal of institutional and political change.' If you will reflect, you will see there is quite a bit of difference in the official objectives of the programs that were funded by OEO and what the EOC is dealing with.

"In the 'Overall Finding,' and under 'Capacity': 'The agency has focused on building the capacity in program management and administration to develop community organization and leadership among the poor for the specific purposes of institutional and political change and on building the capacity to mobilize human resources among the poor. As a by-product in specific programs, the EOC has built some capacity for self-help and development of programs for elimination of specific causes of poverty. It has deliberately not developed any capacity for planning or training though implementation of these objectives was required by OEO in special conditions to the last EOC grant.' This is the official investigation and evaluation."

I had no disagreements with what Chafin was reading, being the first to admit that political and institutional change was, in my opinion, the primary objective of the EOC. However, Chafin knew that a vast majority of people were opposed to poor people's participation in the political decision-making process. The Fair Elections Committee and the Education Committee were prime examples of poor people's groups effecting political and institutional change within the county. He evidently felt that this would be good material to give to Congressman Kee and Senator Byrd because both had accused the EOC of participating in political activity.

For another five or ten minutes, Chafin continued to read excerpts from the OEO document, and then he concluded by saying, "Mr. Chairman, I could go on and on. It is forty-one pages long, and, rather than read and go into any further detail, I think that the sketches I have read clearly indicate why the County Court should take over the administration of the poverty program."

One witness after another paraded to the stand to testify in behalf of the County Court. Among them was Delphia Meade of Dingess, who had been dismissed as Head Start cook by the local community action group and, once dismissed, had quickly shifted her allegiance back to Della Wellman. Della had escorted her to the hearing. In her closing statement, Delphia shouted to the audience, "I have never seen nothing straight in the EOC bunch myself, and especially Huey Perry and Leah Curry. They act like they run the federal government. They never done nothing but lie and undermine people from the beginning. Huey Perry is a liar from the top of his head to the bottom of his foot!"

Other personal attacks on EOC staff members came from several of the County Court's witnesses. We were all accused of fomenting unrest and being involved in political activity. Noah and T. I. found the session particularly enjoyable. Occasionally, they would look at each other and grin, especially when EOC personalities were being attacked. Finally, their hour was up, and the community action people could give their response.

Hamilton was somewhat confused about the speakers, and he asked me to come forward. I explained that we had made no prior arrangements for speakers, but, because I was there, I would speak. The crowd was quiet as I began.

"I think the question here today does not involve the process in which the County Court takes over the poverty agency, but rather why the County Court and the local political machine of this county wish to take it over." I looked straight at Hamilton, but he did not glance my way. I continued, "I personally feel the County Court couldn't care less about the progress of the Head Start Program, the Home Improvement Program, and the other programs administered by our agency. What they would like to have is the one million two hundred thousand dollars so that their patronage system can be perpetuated. The money is needed for their political hacks."

There was considerable applause from the audience, and Hamilton rapped for order.

"They wish to suppress the voices of the people. Three

years ago, there was no voice, only a county dictatorship, and now, three years later, that dictatorship has been weakened by the articulate poor who are, for the first time in the county's history, challenging the very existence of this political system in Appalachia."

Again there was applause, and the chairman rapped his gavel.

I concluded by saying, "The final decision as to who will operate the poverty program in Mingo County will be left up to the Office of Economic Opportunity in Washington. The County Court will not be able to take over your program by the route they are going."

What I had said was a bluff, but I was willing to go out on a limb, for I could see nothing to lose. As I moved toward my seat, many people extended their hands. Others patted me on the back. I felt proud that I had said what I did in front of Noah and his group.

Herb Meade was already talking by the time I sat down.

"In my estimation, this is the only democratic process that the underprivileged in Mingo County has ever had anything to do with. I think the County Court wishes to take over the EOC in Mingo County because they are afraid not to, for fear it will destroy them. They've got petitions here. If it is necessary, we can get people here by the dozens to stand up and tell you that they were lied to to get their name on a piece of paper. As far as I am concerned, rather than see the poverty money given to such an agency as the County Court and be used to prostitute the poor people in Mingo County and further enslave them, get it out of Mingo County and get it to some place where it will do some good."

Again there was applause. Hamilton banged his gavel

and shouted at the crowd, "I might say that the other group did not applaud or anything of that kind, so we are following the same procedure right on through. Now you can be satisfied with what your representatives are saying without—"

He could not be heard over the crowd, and he stopped in frustration. Finally, he yelled again, "You are taking up your own time, and that's the only thing you're doing."

Chester Brown had made his way to the front, and, once the people saw him in the witness stand, they became silent.

"We, the community action group of Browning Fork, Stafford District, Mingo County, West Virginia, give the following reasons why we believe it is against the well-being of the poor people of Mingo County for the Mingo County Court to take over the management of the EOC in Mingo County," Chester spoke out firmly. "Number one— the honesty and the integrity of the present members of the Mingo County Court is under questioning and charges of wrongdoing asking proceedings for ouster from office have been filed in court. Hearing is now pending.

"Number two—we, as citizens of Mingo County know that politics has always come first and the services of the citizens second.

"Number three—under the present management of the EOC, the poor people has found leadership they have confidence in. Before the present EOC was established in Mingo County, the county was run more on the plans of Russia, not the United States Constitution. Some very few from each district recommended whether a person should have consideration from the County Court and other agencies under their control."

187

Chester spoke less than a minute, but he got his message across. Leah Curry was next to continue the attack. "This is a developmental program," she said. "The elimination of poverty in Mingo County is not something which can be done in twenty-four hours. The stages of the development of the total community action program have been brief when one considers the social and economic conditions and injustices which have been prevalent for scores of years. The system which controls the county has also been prevalent for scores of years. It is important to know that one of the largest payrolls in the county is controlled by local and state government. Employment based upon one's potential and ability is not a part of the system. There are thousands of people in Mingo County who are not part of the system but who want to correct it.

"The creation of OEO and the organization of the Mingo County EOC brought a new hope for deliverance of the poor. Maximum feasible participation of the poor was taken seriously by the Mingo County EOC, and it is still taken seriously. A frequent topic of discussion among community action people is always 'How can we get more people involved to solve our problems?' Some call it a movement; others call it a spirit. I have no name, but, whatever it is, it is here to stay. We believe in democracy for all of the people, and, because of this belief, community action makes sense.

"If one is capable of understanding the background of the past, it is not at all difficult to understand why the Mingo County Court would like to create a new antipoverty agency. President Johnson stated last week at a conference on education, meeting at the State Department, that the country is undergoing rapid change, and change is rarely comfortable to any of us. Many of the poor people in our county have become impatient with the pace of change, and they wish to transform the system while others in power cling tenaciously to things as they are. This is the story of Mingo County. The people have worked hard and long to make changes, and changes have been made, or we wouldn't be here today. It has caused ripples in the stream which has flowed so smoothly for years, and the County Court today is making an effort to smooth the water."

I congratulated Leah as she came back to her seat: "Very eloquently spoken."

Our hour was almost over when James Washington began his comments. The audience listened intently.

"I can't conceive of anyone living in Mingo County old enough to vote that has been here for at least one year that can conceive of any type of program run by the County Court that is free of politics. I just don't believe that anyone here can be that dumb. I, for one, don't believe in it, and then, on the other hand, I am not going to get up and tell you how good I am. I believe that I have been around Mingo County most of my life and most of the people know me, and I have, at one time, been a part of the system. You are looking at a person that has sold his vote years ago. You are looking at a person that has worked as a precinct worker in the election years ago, and, when I tell you what is wrong, you are looking at a person that knows what he is talking about.

"It makes me feel good to rub heads with dedicated people, and I think in a way it kindly brings out the best in me, because some of the people that I have been connected with in the EOC, particularly like Miss Curry, and people like Huey Perry, of all people, have the good of the poor and common people at heart. Through this poverty program is a means where some semblance of dignity has been given to the poor people. They have a program whereby they have a voice. They can have a voice in shaping its policies. They can vote on the policy of what's done and what's not.

"I know I have different opinions, and, if I have a different opinion than Mr. Perry, I tell him as quick as I do anybody else, and I will say that that is the one thing about this poverty program that I believe that these politicians don't like—this new-found independence for the poor people. When they hold up their heads and begin to walk with some dignity and tell off anybody that steps on their toes, I don't believe they like that, and this is one more power grab to perpetuate their system here in Mingo County."

The audience was somber as Washington concluded, and Hamilton announced that time was up. Altogether, twelve people had spoken in behalf of the EOC.

Hamilton now motioned for Artis to come closer, and they conferred for about ten seconds before Hamilton, looking over his glasses, said, "Ladies and gentlemen, after consulting with Mr. Artis, the County Court feels it can handle the poverty program, since it has handled various million dollar projects here in the county, and we have voted unanimously to take over the Mingo EOC. The meeting is now adjourned."

Noah, T. I., and a host of deputy sheriffs followed Hamilton and Artis into the judge's chambers, an office suite adjacent to the courtroom.

As the community people went out the opposite end of the courtroom, several of the women were wiping away tears of frustration and anger. Although the community action groups had submitted statements signed by their memberships that they would not participate in a County Court–administered poverty program, the two-man panel had totally ignored what the people had said. Delphia Meade was the only low income person to testify in behalf of the court.

Only two obstacles stood in the way of the politicians now—a legal interpretation of the West Virginia antipoverty law concerning the eligibility of county courts and the governor's signature.

Later, I went to the judge's chamber to secure a copy of the proceedings from the court recorder. "Well, we sure put it over on them," I overheard Harry Artis saying to T. I. and Noah. "Didn't we? They only had twelve to testify, and we had fourteen. That's enough to take it over right there."

About that time, Noah noticed my presence and came immediately to the desk of the court recorder to ask, "What's he want?"

The recorder explained, "Only a copy of the hearing."

"Yeah, Noah," I replied, "don't get nervous. You got everything you wanted today. Unfortunately, you don't have the agency yet, and, in my opinion, you'll never get it." I spoke loudly enough for the entire group to hear, and, before Noah had a chance to reply, I walked out of the room. But I wasn't feeling as sure as I hoped my voice sounded.

14

The outcome of the public hearing did not dampen the hopes of the Mingo County Citizens Committee for Education in its efforts to obtain free hot lunches for the low income students of the county. This committee, made up of delegates from all the community action groups, had first approached the Board of Education in September, 1967. At that time, Jerry Chafin had already signed the Elementary and Secondary Education Act proposal, which indicated that the EOC and all its related groups were satisfied with the various programs outlined in the proposal. The Board of Education used this action as an excuse not to fund a free hot lunch program.

When committee members first attempted to meet with Hershel Morgan, the superintendent, they had to wait forty-five minutes in a supply room that was also used for garbage disposal. The forty members were irate because of this treatment and because of the superintendent's lack of concern over hot lunches. However, Morgan did agree to see a delegation of eight of them at the next regular session of the board.

In Mingo County, it was not customary for interested

citizens to attend Board of Education meetings. In fact, the board always met in a small office in which there was hardly enough space for the five members and Morgan's office staff. However, the eight members of the committee were permitted to crowd in. They presented a four-page proposal prepared in the meantime, asking for a free hot lunch program using ESEA funds to supplement the existing U.S. Department of Agriculture funds already allocated for the county's lunch program. According to research done by the committee, an additional $100,000 could provide free lunches for the poor. The president of the Board of Education, Fred Shewey, one of the county's more affluent citizens, said that the proposal would be taken under advisement and that an answer would be relayed by Superintendent Morgan—perhaps within a week.

Shewey then criticized the committee's recent newspaper publicity. In a letter to the editor of the local newspaper, the committee chairman, Patricia White, had explained that the committee was concerned with (1) limited bus transportation, (2) unsafe drinking water, (3) inadequate teaching facilities, (4) the high cost of workbooks, (5) overcrowded classrooms, (6) the need for kindergartens in the public schools, (7) the shortage of education specialists in such areas as speech therapy, art, and music, and (8) the lack of funds for a free hot lunch program.

Lafe P. Ward, the county's assistant prosecuting attorney, sided with his associate, Shewey, in denouncing the concerns, saying that "the publicity has caused apprehension at large among the people of this county" and that it was irresponsible of the group "to give publicity to something of this nature unless they were prepared to approach the problem."

Although they did not receive any encouragement at the Board of Education meeting, the committee members continued to study local school problems and to meet with parents. On several occasions, they also met with officials of the West Virginia State Department of Education. They vowed to pursue the free hot lunch program once the ESEA program for 1968 was redrawn.

In the late summer of 1968, there was much discussion concerning the strategies that would be used against the Board of Education if it once again refused to include the hot lunch program in its ESEA proposal. This time, there were new considerations. If Floyd was to take over the EOC, he would eventually be able to capture the school board. Its members knew that, and feared it. The EOC needed all the support it could get from agencies such as the school board to oppose the take-over by the County Court. There had been some indication that the school board was willing to draft a letter of support for the existing EOC if the Committee for Education's demands for free hot lunches was dropped. But the issue was too important for compromise. It was decided to invite Robert Marcum, the ESEA county coordinator, to the next Commission meeting, at the end of the month, to discuss the new ESEA proposal. If the Board of Education once again refused the committee's proposal, additional action would be taken. A massive student strike by all low income students was discussed as one alternative.

Marcum, who had originally been a member of the Commission but had quit when Chafin was ousted, accepted the invitation. Surprisingly, he announced that the Board of Education would provide for free hot lunches within its new ESEA proposal provisions. He indicated that he could not specify the amount to be allocated, because the proposal was still in the process of being written, but that it would be ample to meet the needs of the county. He invited the Committee for Education to submit any recommendations that it would like to make and said that the recommendations would be used in drafting the final proposal. For a brief moment, it appeared that the Mingo County Board of Education was now willing to work with the committee and avoid the publicity that would certainly come if the conflict continued.

Herb Meade speculated, "The only thing I can figure out is that the Board of Education wants a united effort this November against Floyd. You know, this is the first time in twelve years that the local Republicans have put out a complete ticket against the Democrats. They know we are all going to vote for the local Republicans, especially the two that are running for the County Court."

Others agreed with Herb. Besides, two members of the Board of Education were Republicans, and they had close friends running for county offices. Noah had opposed the board in the May election, and now was their chance to oppose Noah's slate.

In early September, the contents of the hot lunch proposal were made public. Morgan had agreed to set aside $32,000 of the ESEA monies to feed all the students whose family incomes did not exceed $900 per year. We could not believe what we read. This was a blatant insult to the EOC and the Committee for Education. To believe that a child did not need a free lunch if his parents' income exceeded $75 per month was inhuman.

I did not wait for the committee to call a meeting but called a special meeting of all community groups, including the Committee for Education and the Fair Elections Committee. All were astonished and angered at the board's proposal.

Hol Hannah, chairman of the Dingess Community Action Group, said, "There's just one thing left for us to do, and that's call a strike. We'll start it in Dingess for next Monday morning."

There was unanimous agreement. I explained that to call a strike and to implement an effective strike were two entirely different things, adding, "If you call a strike, and the parents don't cooperate, then you have weakened your position to negotiate with the Board of Education."

Jim Marcum, also from Dingess, suggested, "Don't you think it would be better to hold a community meeting at Dingess and invite all the parents of low income students, and let's see how they feel about the matter?"

Hol said, "You've got a good point there, Jim. Let's meet Saturday night, and, if it looks good, we will call a strike at the Dingess grade school for Monday. Can the EOC staff come over Saturday and help us get the people informed?"

"We will not only have EOC staff but all the volunteers from other parts of the county who are interested in this issue," I said.

Practically all the leaders of the Committee for Education agreed to help, as well as members of the Fair Elections Committee. The plan was to go door to door and explain to the people the position the Board of Education had taken on the proposed hot lunch program.

The efforts paid off. On Saturday night, the community building was packed to capacity, and there were people standing on the outside. Several had missed the regular

Saturday night church revival to attend the meeting. Hol called on me to review what had happened regarding the ESEA fund. I explained that the Mingo County Board of Education received each year approximately $700,000 in federal money to develop programs for the disadvantaged. The guidelines for this particular program required that the school board enlist the ideas of poor people by establishing an advisory group made up of 50 per cent low income parents before programs were developed. So far, the board had totally rejected parent participation.

The crowd listened very carefully as I continued, "It is my opinion that a large portion of the monies are wasted. For example, thousands of dollars have been spent on all types of educational instructional equipment that has never been used. You will find this equipment stored in every closet of every school room in this county collecting dust. Not one program in the past three years has been developed exclusively for the poor. I ask the Board of Education, 'How can a child learn on an empty stomach?' "

The crowd roared approval.

"According to the figures compiled by our office, and based upon the applications made for assistance from the EOC emergency food program," I continued, "there are thirteen hundred students in need of a free lunch. Morgan claims less than five hundred—and then only if your family income is less than $75 per month."

"To hell with Morgan!" an irate poor parent, Anderson Baisden, shouted from the rear of the room.

I continued to explain that the Committee for Education had worked for a hot lunch for almost a year without success and that I believed it was now time for all the parents to lend their support to the effort.

"Thank you, Mr. Perry," Hol said, looking down at the floor. "We met in Williamson this Thursday, and we decided to strike the schools until the board agrees to a hot lunch program that is acceptable to the parents."

There was loud applause. Many yelled, "Let's strike!"

Hol hesitated a few minutes while the people talked. Then he continued, "When we strike, we've got to stick. There ain't no backing down. Now, if you think you can't hold out to the very end, then don't agree with us."

He stepped up on a bench so he could overlook the crowd. "I want to see now how many of you will join the strike. Hold your hands up."

Practically everyone in the room raised his hand in support, and there was a wild emotional outburst. "We'll show that damned Morgan!" I heard one man shout.

Hol asked for silence. He then said that the strike would begin in Dingess Monday and would spread to other schools Tuesday. The strategy was to strike first those schools where community action was strongest and gradually involve other schools.

On Monday, September 9, more than 300 of the 465 students boycotted the Dingess grade school. Parents, carrying signs demanding free hot lunches for their children, appeared early in front of the school. Drivers delivering bread, soft drinks, and milk were turned back by the pickets.

As quoted in the evening paper, the principal of the school, Bob Cline, made an attempt to play down the effectiveness of the strike. He reported that 80 per cent of the students were in school and indicated that another 10 per cent were absent because of illness or injury, while the remaining 10 per cent had remained away from school for some reason other than the strike. Both Cline and Superintendent Morgan said that they had not been officially informed of the pupil strike, although Morgan made no public statement.

The following morning, the *Charleston Gazette's* lead story concerned the student strike in Mingo. It explained in detail that the controversy was centered around the $75-per-month income cutoff as proposed by the Board of Education. It also gave an accurate statement of the number of students who had missed school at Dingess.

Within three days, eight other schools had joined the walkout. All efforts to persuade Morgan and the Board of Education to negotiate proved futile. On September 11, another community meeting held at Dingess was attended by a larger crowd than had turned out for the original Saturday night meeting. Several representatives from other striking schools were present. So was Bob Curry, and the crowd demanded a statement from him.

Bob knew that he could not involve the Office of Economic Opportunity in the dispute. At the same time, he felt obligated to support the strikers. He looked at me as if to say, "What do I do?"

I encouraged him to speak and whispered, "You can always deny tomorrow anything you say, if it gets you into trouble."

Before Bob had finished, he had publicly criticized Morgan and the Board of Education for their failure to respond to the needs of the poor. He was interrupted several times by applause and had come very close to having the OEO involved when he was interrupted by a disturbance near the entrance of the building. Two young women from the community, employed as teachers' aides at the Dingess grade school, were attempting to tape Bob's speech with a portable tape recorder they had sneaked into the room. Once they were discovered, they were chased from the building to their automobile by several other women from the Dingess community. Most of the people at the meeting hurried outside to watch.

"Break their damn necks, the dirty spies!" one woman yelled.

The aides had locked themselves in their automobile, which was now encircled by the angry women of Dingess. Seeing that there was a potential for violence, I suggested that it would be better for the women to disperse. They immediately stepped aside, and the aides drove away. Everyone laughed at the incident and went back into the building.

The next day the two aides obtained warrants before Justice of the Peace Dewey Thompson for the arrest of the nine women involved in the incident, charging them with unlawfully and feloniously conspiring together for the purpose of inflicting punishment and bodily injury. After they had been arrested by state policemen, the women refused bond and declared they would go to jail for the hot lunch program. They were later tried by the same magistrate who had issued the warrants, and, as the community people had expected, all were found guilty. The defendants appealed their cases to the Mingo County Grand Jury and were freed on certified bonds of $500 each.

If this incident was planned by school officials to dampen the effect of the student strike, it must have been disappointing. During the next three days, an additional twelve grade schools joined the strike.

Superintendent Morgan made his first public statement

on September 12, when he told the *Charleston Gazette,* "We drew up a proposal to feed five hundred children. Of course, there are less than that who need it. There are definitely less than that!" (Mingo County had a school enrollment of 11,223.)

Morgan continued, "Huey Perry came here one day and spent from half an hour to forty-five minutes discussing the proposal, and we had an advisory committee on which the EOC was represented. We used the EOC's figures. They said there were five hundred families who couldn't pay for lunches, and we drew up a program for five hundred children."

Morgan further stated, "Frankly, we still don't think Perry's five hundred–family figure is correct. We don't believe Mingo County has five hundred families which earn less than $75 a month. Why, if they were that poor, they'd be on welfare, wouldn't they? And welfare families get more than $75 a month.

"Huey Perry is a former teacher in this county. It is inconceivable that a teacher would advocate that students stay away from classes and miss the opportunity to obtain a formal education, when it is generally agreed in the United States that the crying need in our times is for each and every child to get a good education," Morgan concluded.

We complained bitterly to the West Virginia State Department of Education, which was in the process of reviewing the Mingo ESEA proposal, about the board's $75-a-month guideline. Shortly thereafter, we got the first of two breaks. Clarence Brock, assistant state superintendent of schools in charge of federal programs, said, "The rigid and restrictive guidelines of the board's proposal must be replaced with a flexible sliding income scale, to give families with several children as much consideration as those with one or two."

After the announcement by Brock, the Committee for Education met with the strike committee and compiled a five-point proposal, which was submitted to the Board of Education. It was our first offering since the strike had begun. The five points were: (1) Allow the State Department of Education to establish eligibility guidelines based on the number of children in school per family; (2) provide an additional $15,000 in ESEA money, in which case the Mingo County EOC would provide an additional $15,000 through its emergency food program, bringing the free hot lunch program total to $70,000; (3) establish a simplified procedure for certifying eligible children; (4) forbid reprisals by principals or teachers against any children who remain out of school; and (5) have each principal meet once a month with a committee from the community action group to report the number of children certified for a free hot lunch and to give a program report.

The second break came on the eighth day of the strike, when the *Charleston Gazette* criticized Morgan and the position of the school board in an editorial:

> Matters appear to be going from bad to worse in the current dispute involving the Mingo County school system, and the reason seems to be the failure—or refusal—of the Board of Education to do what it should be doing with respect to the school lunch program.
>
> The issue is over how many children are to be given free lunches. The school board has drawn up a proposal to feed 500 children. But the Mingo County Economic Opportunity Commission (E.O.C.), a federally financed anti-poverty agency, contends there are at least 1,300 children who need free lunches and aren't getting them.

There the matter stands, and the poor people are so aroused that they're keeping their children out of school. Large numbers of pupils remain absent from sixteen Mingo County schools, with the strike for food going into its eighth day. . . .

Considering the importance of education, particularly to those seeking economic betterment, school authorities have a point in arguing that parents are doing no service to their children in keeping them out of school. . . .

But there is something to be said also for the position of E.O.C. director Huey Perry and the parents, who contend the children can't get anything out of school if they must sit through classes all day nursing empty stomachs.

And on this score, the school board is in a dreadfully indefensible position.

Under the board's proposal, only children of families which earn $75 or less per month are eligible for free lunches —and it is utterly ridiculous to suggest that no other children are in need of a hot meal.

Furthermore, the State Department of Education has said the Mingo lunch proposal is improperly drawn and must be revised. Clarence Brock, Assistant State Superintendent of Schools in charge of federal programs, said last week the rigid and restrictive guidelines of the board's proposal must be replaced with a flexible, sliding income scale to "give families with several children as much consideration as those with one or two."

But even this has so far failed to move the Mingo board, and school authorities also have given a cool reception to the E.O.C.'s offer of $15,000 to expand the lunch program.

Perry makes a persuasive case in support of his estimate that at least 1,300 children in Mingo County are in need of free school lunches.

Using the board's guidelines and singling out children of families with less than $75 a month income, Perry said he found only 116 children who would have been eligible in a sampling of 892 Mingo families who have applied for help from the E.O.C.'s emergency food program in the past several months.

"Yet," he added, "all these families—with 1,828 children among them—obviously need aid desperately because they applied to us for emergency help. . . ."

It is noteworthy that the highest income considered by Perry in establishing eligibility for free lunches is $225 a month, or $2,700 a year. This must be ranked as conservative in estimating the need, considering that the national poverty standard is $3,000 per year. . . .

In the meantime, the hot lunch proponents had organized an anti-school levy group and petitioned the Board of Education for representation in the polling precincts. The cry now was "No hot lunch, no school levy." The levy election, scheduled to be held on October 15, was to provide for partial payment of teachers' salaries, school building maintenance, and school construction. There had never been opposition to a school levy before, and the local board had always appointed election officials without opposition. But, because a levy election required 60 per cent approval for passage, the poor believed that they had the votes to defeat it.

An ultimatum was sent to Morgan and each school board member, explaining the intentions of the poor to defeat the levy unless a suitable hot lunch program was implemented. The following day, I received a telephone call from Fred Shewey. This was the first contact between the EOC and the Board of Education. Shewey indicated that he would like to get together with me but, fearing that the press would be involved, did not want to meet in Williamson. He suggested that I meet him about ten miles outside the Williamson city limits, beside the road at the junction of U.S. Route 52 and State Route 65. He would drive twenty-five miles from his home in Kermit, a small municipality at the northern end of the county.

I arrived about five minutes early and awaited him. It was an unusual place to hold a discussion, but the only thing I wanted was a suitable hot lunch program, and the location of the meeting was irrelevant.

When he arrived, he parked his car adjacent to mine. He nodded his head, smiling, took a piece of paper from his glove compartment, and came over to my car. "Hi, Perry," he said, as he extended his hand.

I returned the greeting. Like me, he was plainly nervous and wanted to go immediately to the issue. I waited for him to raise the question.

"Perry, do you think we can settle this?"

"I don't see any problem at all, if the board and Morgan will be realistic with their proposal. Our objection is to the $75-per-month cutoff and the number of children you propose to feed."

"Well, you know this thing is really giving the whole county a black eye. All this bad publicity is just not good for us," he said as he fumbled with the piece of paper he had taken from his glove compartment. "You know, Morgan is a stubborn man, but there is one thing about him— he is as honest as the day is long, and it has always been our policy to back him. But this thing has gotten so bad. We would like to keep everything as quiet as possible until we settle it."

"If it can be settled," I replied, "I think the publicity would stop immediately."

"Yeah, I think you are right. But we are so far apart, I don't know how we can reach an agreement without it looking like the board had to bend all the way. What do you think?" he asked as he glanced across at me.

I did not have an immediate solution but assured him I would be happy to issue a joint statement if and when the strike was settled. His tension appeared to be eased somewhat.

"What about the levy? Would your group withdraw its opposition?" he asked, as he opened the piece of paper he had been holding and glanced at it. I could see that it was a copy of the ultimatum the anti–school levy group had sent.

"There is no question in my mind that the group would be happy to withdraw opposition if the strike can be settled," I answered.

"You know," he said next, "we are out to get Noah, and we want to give him as much opposition as possible in November. We just can't do it if we are involved in this kind of problem. I'll tell you what I am going to do, Perry. Now, this is just me—I don't know how the rest of the board feels—but I am going to meet with Morgan in a few minutes and see if we can get this settled. I'll let you know something tomorrow."

Assessing the roadside meeting as I drove back to Cinderella, I felt that we were in an excellent position. I had no reason to doubt Shewey's intentions, and I was reasonably sure that the other board members would vote with him. However, I decided to avoid any premature announcement to the community people until I heard again from Shewey.

He called promptly at 9:00 the following morning. "Well, Perry, I think we can settle this. I got Morgan to raise the guidelines."

"That's great!" I said, meaning it.

"Yeah, he has agreed to raise them to $105 a month."

My enthusiasm changed to disappointment. Once again, I could not believe the board's position. "You mean anyone above $105 per month, regardless of the number of children in the family, is ineligible?"

"I guess so," he replied. "We have to cut it off somewhere."

"Well, if that is the best you can do, we are as far away from a settlement as ever," I told him. "I am sure the community people will reject the offer."

He interrupted, "But I thought this would be acceptable."

"No, no," I answered, "it will have to be based on a sliding scale according to the number of children in the family."

"Well, I am disappointed at your reaction," Shewey replied, "but this is the best we can do."

The following day I met with the strike committee and related the board's recent proposal. It was unanimously rejected. The group then decided to intensify its efforts and spread the two-week-old strike to all of Mingo's forty schools, including the high schools. The following Monday, more than three thousand students were absent, although the superintendent's office continued to issue news releases claiming that everything was normal in the county's schools.

By Tuesday morning, strenuous efforts on the part of the truant officers, teachers, and other school personnel to get the students back in the classrooms began to have some success. The number of students remaining out that day dropped to 2,100. There was concern among several of the strike leaders that people were beginning to give up, and, comparing the two days' strike totals, I was inclined to agree. We believed that we were close to a settlement, if only we could get the message across to the people without weakening our position with the board, but this seemed impossible, and, if more students showed up in class on Wednesday, it was certain that the board would refuse to negotiate further. At 1:00 P.M. on Tuesday, the strike leaders assembled, and we reviewed our progress in all areas of the county. The conclusion was grim: The Board of Education was wearing down the resistance of the striking students, and two more days would finish us.

Having listened carefully to the reports, I suggested that we immediately end the strike and begin our own hot lunch program, using money from our emergency food program for a twenty-day period. We would state its purpose as being to prove emphatically to the Board of Education that there were 1,300 students who were in need of a free lunch. It would keep the issue alive and give us time to work out new strategies. Because this was the only alternative presented, the group agreed, and I called Len Slaughter, OEO District Director, for permission to use up to $6,000 of emergency food money to pay for the lunches.

In unprecedented time, I received from the OEO a telegram giving us permission to proceed. We immediately issued a press release calling an end to the strike and, at the same time, announcing the emergency lunch program and stating that efforts to defeat the school levy would continue.

Implementing the EOC lunch program created as much controversy as the strike itself. In many instances, volunteers who were stationed at each school to determine the eligibility of the students were denied entrance to the school by the principals. Other principals refused to accept EOC checks. Stations were later set up off the school grounds, and volunteers gave the money directly to the students, thereby prompting an immediate letter to Senator Byrd from one school official, charging the EOC with mismanagement of poverty funds. But, within two days, more than 1,500 students were certified for free lunches, and the results were announced in the state newspapers.

Our charges of noncooperation brought countercharges from Superintendent Morgan and the county nutrition supervisor, Julia Hatfield. Morgan said, "School officials are cooperating in the emergency free lunch program set up by the EOC, but we are using our own methods to implement it."

Mrs. Hatfield added, "Several schools could not begin this supplemental program the first day, because the milk trucks do not deliver on Wednesdays, and there was not sufficient notice as to how many children to prepare for. When a Class A lunch is served in our schools, milk must be served with it in order to comply with federal standards."

We were pleased with the initial effect our hot lunch program was having upon the school administrators. They remained on the defensive by continuing to deny that there were hungry school children in Mingo. But we felt the need to exert more pressure. One possibility was to intensify our efforts to organize a union of the county school bus drivers.

Our attempt a year before had failed. Many of the drivers were suspicious of unions because of the United Mine Workers' ineffectiveness in dealing with the problems of Mingo's displaced coal miners in the early 1950's. Within a year after the miners had lost their jobs, the union withdrew all benefits. For the miners, this meant the loss of their hospitalization cards and their retirement benefits. The UMW in Mingo was looked upon as an instrument of the coal operators. However, we had not considered the organization of a union a dead issue and had revived our efforts with the beginning of the school term. Potential leaders among the bus drivers had been identified, and we had induced them to meet with a representative of Amalgamated Transit, an international union of drivers. The union members who were present for this meeting, convinced that there was a need to establish a local in Mingo, had been talking with the school bus drivers on an individual basis. I personally believed the timing to be right for a second organizational effort now. If the hot lunch issue could be combined with a strike of the bus drivers, it would place a tremendous amount of pressure on the Board of Education.

We got in touch with the Amalgamated Transit representative in Charleston and scheduled a meeting for the following Saturday night with all the Mingo bus drivers. Most of them turned up, and, after emotional speeches by the union representative and Laverne Copley, the driver who had been selected by the group to act as its president, they decided not only to organize but also to strike.

On Monday morning, all fifty-eight Mingo County school bus drivers were off the job, and more than 80 per cent of the students were absent from the county's schools. The drivers sent a registered letter to Morgan, demanding a meeting with the Board of Education to work out an agreement whereby the board would recognize Amalgamated Transit as the official bargaining agent for the bus drivers. The struggle was expected to be a difficult one, for all the board members were antiunion. Shewey had previously had serious problems with the National Labor Relations Board, and his attitude toward organized labor was well known. A strike of public employees was something new for Mingo County, and we waited eagerly for reaction from the board.

It came as an editorial in the local paper, which had always been an ardent supporter of the Board of Education. The editorial read, in part:

> The educational process in Mingo County has been disrupted somewhat since September 9, and even more so since Monday of this week.
>
> The Mingo E.O.C. backed a walkout of students for several days, and still has a running feud with the Board of Education over the hot lunch program, putting in its own program at most schools.
>
> And now the school bus drivers have gone on strike, for how long, nobody knows right now.
>
> Everyone around the country is always making fun of the Appalachian region, anyway, and the best way for us to overcome such a stigma is through education. And the boys and girls can't get an education when their programs are continually being interrupted.
>
> We're not here to pass judgment on the E.O.C., the bus drivers, or the Board of Education. But we do know that something has to be done—and quickly.
>
> We've read of the teachers' strike, the student boycotts, and all the trouble they've had in the big city schools, but this is something new for Mingo County, and it is the *Daily News*' urgent plea for the educational process to be returned to normal, with the E.O.C., the school bus drivers, and members of the Board of Education sitting down and working something out.

I interpreted this editorial as being an overture from the Board of Education to negotiate a settlement. That evening, I called Laverne Copley and told him to be ready to negotiate. If the editorial could be interpreted as official board policy, there was no doubt that he would be approached soon.

The following day, I received a call from Shewey, who wanted to know whether a meeting would be useful. He indicated that he had a new proposal to make and would be willing this time to come to Cinderella.

He arrived at 4:00 P.M., we greeted each other, and he immediately handed me a single sheet of paper.

"Can you accept these?" he asked.

On the paper was a set of guidelines based on a sliding income scale that was almost identical to the ones we had originally submitted.

I said I thought we could accept but inquired, "What about the school bus strike?"

"We're settling that today, also. The board has agreed to recognize the union. You weren't behind that, too, were you?"

I grinned, signed the agreement, and gave a copy to Donna for the files.

15

While the poor people of Mingo County were absorbed in the hot lunch dispute, little attention was given to the fact that, during a special session of the state legislature, Governor Hulett Smith had placed on the agenda antipoverty legislation allowing county courts the authority to take over antipoverty programs. (An assistant state attorney had previously ruled that county courts were ineligible because they could not delegate authority, and all poverty agencies had to consist of at least one-third poor people.) The emergency legislation was sponsored in the state Senate by Noah Floyd and in the House of Delegates by T. I. Varney. Cleo Jones, the Fair Elections Committee's legal counsel and a delegate from Kanawha County, blasted the bill, but it passed the House by a sixty to twenty-six vote.

Jones later said, "There was no emergency whatsoever for this bill. It was a move for politicians in southern counties to take over poverty programs so they could put poor people in line. The Mingo EOC has been regarded as a national model by the OEO for the poor's war on poverty.

What worries me is that the efforts of the poor people in Mingo County to correct the problems will be killed by the same people who caused them."

With the general election less than three weeks away, the Fair Elections Committee again intensified its efforts to bring a fair election to Mingo. As a result of the committee's work over the past year, the official registration was now under 19,000—a far cry from the 29,000 registered to vote in 1966. Again, requests went out to the Justice Department begging for federal observers, as during the previous primary election, and again it appeared that the pleas would be in vain.

The poor people were rallying behind the Republican candidates who had pledged to reverse the County Court's decision to take over the poverty agency. However, very few expected the Republicans to win. During the past thirty years, the Republican candidates for local office had never polled more than two thousand votes, while the Democrats usually ran up a total of twelve thousand to fourteen thousand votes.

On Thursday, October 24, members of the Fair Elections Committee and EOC staff members were able to secure affidavits from several of the voters who had been bought by the Floyd machine. Absentee voting had begun in early October, and employees of the county and the state were once again busy hauling voters to the courthouse. In the presence of election observers, they were openly voted.

One such case involved Earn Davis, Sr., who made the following statement to Fair Elections Committee workers and, later, to the Federal Bureau of Investigation. In his own words, he related how Ike Newsome had bought his family's votes:

On Wednesday evening, October 9, 1968, Ike Newsome stopped at my house and told me if I could get Junior and Lois to go and vote an absentee ballot, he would pay them $5.00 each and would pick us up at 10:00 a.m. Thursday, October 10, 1968.

Ike came to our home on Road Branch about 10:00 Thursday morning, October 10, 1968, and told us that there was going to be trouble. He said if we voted an absentee ballot, we wouldn't have to be around.

I told him that I didn't want no trouble and didn't want to be in it, that I'd just as soon go on and vote.

Ike took me and my wife, Evelyn, Earn, Jr., and Lois Jean, and another boy, making five of us, in his car to the courthouse. He had to park the car at the depot, and all of us walked from there to the courthouse. When we got to the courthouse, he took us to Tom Chafin's office where we all sat down. Ike then took us one at a time on the elevator, riding with each of us. He took us to the Circuit Clerk's office and told them we wanted to vote. Ike told me to tell the people in charge that I had to go to Pilgrim's Knob, Virginia. I told Ike I was going to see about the rock dust,* but I didn't say when. He told me to tell them I would be going on election day. I told him I might be gone. That is the reason I voted an absentee ballot—I didn't want to be around any fighting or any trouble.

After we had voted, Ike took us downstairs, and I told him I had to go to the drug store and would meet him back at the car. Me, my wife, Earn, Jr., Lois, and the other boy met Ike at his car at the depot. While we were sitting in the car, Ike gave me some money rolled up. I didn't know how much it was, but I put it in my pocket. When we started down the road, I took it out and saw that there was four five-dollar bills. I gave my wife $10.00 of the money and gave Junior $10.00 for him and Lois. I told Ike, "I didn't come up here for the money; I just came up here to vote, to help you

---

* Silicosis, a lung disease caused by working in the coal mines, is commonly called "rock dust" in Appalachia.

fellers; but if you want to give it to me, I'll take it." I hadn't worked since last January, 1967.

Ike was my boss when I worked under him for the A.F.D.C.U. He kind of drove us a little. He told us then if we didn't vote their way we were liable to be cut off. This was last year; so he knew how I would vote. He told me then that he had me "fouled." I had to then, but I don't now as I'm on Social Security disability.

Another incident was related by Alvin James Estepp, a thirty-three-year-old welfare recipient, who reportedly sold his vote to T. I. Varney.

Ike Newsome talked to me first, about two weeks ago, and said to me, "Why don't you go on up and vote absentee. You don't have to be out of the state to vote an absentee ballot, just out of the county"—or district, one or the other; I don't remember just which one he told me.

Ike Newsome was supposed to pick me up at Vinnie New's house, me and her together. We waited until about 9:30 a.m. on October 14, or a little later than that; then I went down to Earn Davis's house and asked him to bring me to Williamson to vote an absentee ballot. Then we, Earn Davis, Jr., and his wife, and Boyd McNeely, and Delmer Estepp, my brother, all came to Williamson, went across the bridge into Kentucky and parked the pickup truck, then walked back across the bridge to Williamson, West Virginia, to the courthouse.

Me and Boyd McNeely and my brother, Delmer, we stood around about thirty minutes, and then we asked the lady at the desk if Ike Newsome had been there today. She said no. I turned around and saw T. I. Varney coming towards me. I asked him if he had seen Ike Newsome, and he said, "No, why? Do you want to vote an absentee ballot?" And I said yes. Then he said, "Come on; I can take care of you the same as Ike can."

Then me and Roland New, and my wife, who was already

at the courthouse when I got there, along with T. I. Varney, went up the stairs to the second floor of the courthouse to the Circuit Clerk's office; and T. I. said to the woman behind the desk, "Two more voters," and held up two fingers.

Then the woman got the applications and filled them out. She asked me where I was going, and I told her that I was going to Columbus, Ohio, to work, and then I signed the card, then went back in the room to vote.

The man at the desk asked me if I wanted to go back and vote by myself or vote here on the table. I said that I'll just vote here. I need some help; I can't read very good. And then he said, "What are you, Democrat or Republican?" And I said, "I want to vote a straight Democrat vote. I guess I have been one all of my life." And he said, "Well, mark right here."

Then I came out of the room, me and Roland New and my wife. My wife did not vote as I know of. We came down the stairs together and stood around for a few minutes, and T. I. Varney came up to us and reached me and Roland New a five-dollar bill each and told us we had better not stand around, somebody might suspect something, so move on out. So we left the courthouse and went to the truck that was parked in Kentucky and then went home.

William R. Marcum, a fifty-three-year-old ex–coal miner, explained how a deputy sheriff bought his vote:

On October 15, 1968, Morrie Blair contacted me and asked me to vote an absentee ballot in the Circuit Clerk's office in the courthouse; and on October 16, Morrie Blair picked me and my wife, Angeline, up and transported us in his car to Williamson, West Virginia; and upon arriving in Williamson, my wife and I went to the Circuit Clerk's office, where both of us voted absentee ballots; and I gave as my reason for voting an absentee ballot that I planned to be in Wadsworth, Ohio, on election day. I was permitted to vote, and having voted, met Morrie Blair in the hallway on the first floor of the courthouse, and then he took my wife and me to our home in his car. Morrie Blair paid me $10.00 in cash in the courthouse after I had cast an absentee ballot."

Mary Ann Akers told how a state employee approached her:

On October 22, 1968, I was in the Mingo County courthouse getting a drink of water at the fountain when Vurnam "Bum" Davis approached me. He said, "Why don't you go up and vote for me?"

I told him I really didn't want to, but he said he would give me five dollars after I came downstairs, so I finally did. He took me up on the elevator and told me to vote straight Democrat. He said to explain to the Circuit Clerk that I was going to be away from home; so I told him I would be in Lisbon, Ohio, on election day.

After I voted, Bum Davis took me back downstairs. He walked into the sheriff's office and then came out and gave me a five-dollar bill. He asked me if there was anyone I could bring in, and I told him no. He said he would give them five dollars if they would come in.

There were others, like James McNeely's:

Mattie Estepp, my aunt, came down and told me, my wife, and my father, Boyd McNeely, that Ike Newsome would pay us $5.00 for voting, but he couldn't take us till Wednesday, October 16, 1968, because Tuesday was a special election day. Ike Newsome came to my home to get us on Wednesday as planned, but I told him I'd take my own car since we had to take the kids with us.

When we got to the Mingo County courthouse in Williamson, Ike got on the elevator with me and said, "You know how I want you to vote—straight Democrat ticket—but I know you're a Democrat anyhow. I'll be waiting downstairs to pay you." He went on back down in the elevator when I went in to vote.

When I got downstairs after I voted, Ike Newsome walked up to me and said, "Let's go into the men's restroom." After

218

we were in the restroom, Ike Newsome handed me a folded dollar bill and said, "Here's the money." I started to put it in my pocket, and he said, "That's ten dollars for you and your wife." It was a ten-dollar bill. Before we left the rest-room, he asked me if I could get Kelly Gauze's vote, and I asked him if Kelly's wife could vote since she is only twenty, and he said no.

One affidavit involved Jack Webb, brother-in-law to Noah Floyd, who was running for circuit clerk of Mingo, the office responsible for conducting absentee voting. Harry Joe Urban related the story:

On Monday, October 14, 1968, I came to Williamson, West Virginia, on my own, hitchhiking to Williamson from Naugatuck with a stranger, and upon my arrival in Williamson, I visited the Mingo County courthouse, where Jack Webb came to me on the second floor and asked me if I wanted to vote an absentee ballot. He told me he would take care of me, meaning that he would pay me for my vote.

I told him I would, and I went to the Circuit Clerk's office and voted an absentee ballot after telling them that I thought I might be in the hospital on election day. I walked to the first floor of the courthouse and again met Jack Webb. He had agreed to pay $5.00; however, when I went in his of-fice, he took a five-dollar bill out of a desk in the county courtroom and put it in his pocket and gave me three one-dollar bills. I approached him again on Wednesday, October 16, and he gave me another dollar.

The Fair Elections Committee, seizing upon the oppor-tunity to publicly expose the corrupt practice, obtained warrants for the arrest of Delegate T. I. Varney, Ike New-some, Constable Nick Davis, Vurnam Davis, and Morrie Blair, on charges of vote buying. All across the state, news-papers carried the story. The Federal Bureau of Investiga-tion was officially notified of the warrants, and the affidavits were submitted to the Department of Justice in Washington.

When the warrants were issued, Ike, Ike's son, and Constable Nick Davis attempted to persuade the complainants to withdraw their statements. A midnight visit was paid to the home of Alvin Estepp, who later related the incident:

Ike Newsome, his son, and Nick Davis came to my house on October 24, 1968, at about 12:00 midnight and woke me up. Someone hollered, "Hey, Estepp, do you know who this is?"

I said, "No, sir, I don't."

The person said, "This is Ike Newsome."

So I said, "Come on in."

Ike Newsome's son said to me, "I have some papers here that I want you to sign, dropping all charges against Daddy."

I asked what the papers were. He—Ike Newsome's son—said that there were warrants against his daddy for buying votes. He—Ike Newsome's son—then read the paper to me: "I, Alvin James Estepp, hereby withdraw all charges against Daddy."

I then told him I was not signing anything until I checked further and see what this is all about. I then called for my wife to get up out of the bed, which she did. After coming in the room where he was, I asked her to read the paper. Ike Newsome's son had the paper in his hand and was trying to hold it while my wife read it. She asked him to give the paper to her, and she read it, as follows: "I, Alvin James Estepp, withdraw all charges against T. I. Varney." It further stated that I had been approached by strong-arm people passing theirselves as F.B.I.

I then said to them, "That's a goddamned lie! Nobody has been to me and said they are F.B.I. or anything else." My wife at this point stopped reading the paper and reached it back to Ike's son and left the room.

Ike followed her into the bedroom. She later told me he asked her to get me to sign the paper, and she told him that I was a man of my own head and could do what I wanted to do. Then he came back in the room where we were and said to his son and Nick Davis, "Let's go." Then they left the house, and I went back to bed.

Lois Davis told how Ike and his wife, Ida, visited her father in an effort to get the warrants withdrawn:

Ike Newsome and his wife, Ida Newsome, came to our house on October 24, 1968, at about 3.30 P.M. Mrs. Newsome, Ike's wife, called for my mother-in-law, Evelyn Davis, to come out to the car, that she, Ida Newsome, wanted to ask her something. She went out to the car. Then my father-in-law, Earn Davis, Sr., came out of the house to get a bucket of water, and Ike Newsome got out of the car and came up to my father-in-law Earn Davis, Sr., and said to him, "Earn, I thought you and me were friends." And my father-in-law said, "Buddy, you got me in trouble, I had to do something." Ike said, "It's all a bunch of junk that Huey Perry has started. He has started something he cannot finish," and then he said, "I will see you."

Then, last night at about 11:30 p.m., Ike Newsome, his son, and Nick Davis came to our house. My father and mother-in-law was in the bed asleep. What sounded like Ike Newsome called for Earn to get up, he wanted to talk to him. They were all in the kitchen talking—Ike Newsome, his son, Nick Davis, and my father-in-law. Ike was telling Earn that there was nothing to all this mess that Huey Perry had started. Ike said to his son, "Show Earn the paper," but they never did read what the paper said to him as I know of, and I was within eight or ten feet of where they were all talking.

Ike said to Earn, "You sign this paper, and then your wife can sign one, and it will free me of all charges." Then Earn said his wife was in bed asleep. Ike said, "I will wake her up and ask her if she wants to sign the paper."

She first refused to sign it but did later after Earn Davis, her husband, did. Then they left the house and went to their car. I looked out the window, and the light was on in their car. They were laughing.

All the defendants were to appear before Jim Marcum, the justice of the peace who had issued the warrants. Marcum had been a strong advocate of community action and, as a result, his office was boycotted by law enforcement officers. This was his first case in over a year. However, no one believed that the defendants would be prosecuted. Under West Virginia law, they could ask for a change of venue and have the case transferred to a friendly justice of the peace, where it would be thrown out. The Fair Elections Committee was more interested in bringing pressure on the Department of Justice for a full-scale investigation than in attempting local prosecution.

When Governor Smith came to the county two days later to speak before the Noah Floyd machine at a Democratic dinner, he made no mention of the arrests or vote fraud in Mingo. He was substituting for Senator Byrd, who had canceled at the last minute. Smith was introduced by Robert Staker, an attorney whose brother had married Noah's daughter. Staker was running for the office of county judge. He praised the Smith Administration and Smith personally as a "man who has been good for our state and extraordinarily good for Mingo County." No one had expected Smith to choose such an occasion to announce that he had written a letter to the OEO in Washington certifying that the Mingo County Court was qualified to run the antipoverty program. But he did. This announcement received the loudest applause of the evening.

After the dinner, Smith told a local reporter, "It is out of the hands of the OEO now. With my authorization of the County Court to run the antipoverty agency and the fact the County Court has met all requirements connected with such an undertaking, the OEO has no alternative but to give its approval to the County Court."

I was infuriated when I learned of Smith's announcement. When a reporter from the *Charleston Gazette* questioned me the following day, I explained, "I interpret Smith's statement as a strictly political announcement to gain votes for the local Democratic Party. It means that he is opposed to fair elections, free hot lunch programs, and poor people in general. He has thrown them to the lion's den. Smith is a desperate politician who has never made one decision that favors poor people. He is basically opposed to poor people controlling their own lives."

Ironically, on the same day as Smith's announcement, the Fair Elections Committee sent the following letter to Steven J. Pollock, an Assistant U.S. Attorney General in Washington, D.C.:

Since 1966, documented evidence of numerous and diverse instances of election fraud perpetrated in Mingo County, West Virginia, has been submitted to your office on several occasions. Our group, the Mingo County Fair Elections Committee, has already sent you affidavits substantiating the following willful and systematic attempts to unfairly influence and manipulate the outcome of elections and thus deprive the citizens of this county of their right of the franchise by:

(1) *Voter intimidation*: Citizens have been subjected to threats of violence, actual infliction of bodily injury, and threats to their means of livelihood, for the purpose of depriving them of their constitutional right to vote. Most of the threats of violence and economic pressure have come from persons whose duty it is to uphold the law (i.e., constables, deputy sheriffs, justices of the peace and other elected officials). For example, your office has received affidavits documenting the mistreatment of witnesses and intimidation of attorneys which occurred in the Court of Justice of the Peace, Arden Mounts of this county. The latter convicted and fined defendants for violating a law which does not exist and which charges were obviously intended to obstruct and

harass citizens who attempted to correct abuses in the election process. Your office also has affidavits concerning attempted intimidation of citizens engaged in legitimate poll watching activities in this year's primary; for example, the cases of Mr. Sidney Murphy and Mr. Roy Barnhart, who were threatened with violence, and Mr. Barry Griever and Mr. Peter Ellis, who actually were physically assaulted, all four incidents where local *law enforcement* officers violated the law in attempting to deprive the poll watchers of their constitutional rights. These are merely selected cases—you have received other data which demonstrates that this type of voter intimidation is systematic and deliberate.

(2) *Registration fraud*: Election fraud has been perpetrated by elected officials and others through the devices of (a) registration rolls padded with dead persons, persons who have moved away, and persons who for other reasons are not entitled to be on the rolls; (b) intimidation of citizens who try to correct the registration records by public officials; (c) failure to properly inform registrars and other officials whose duty it is to conduct proper purging of the rolls. Your office has extensive lists of persons in several precincts who are listed as voting well after their deaths, of persons registered in Kentucky and also still registered in Mingo. Other affidavits document that Fair Elections Committee members were refused access to the registration books by the responsible local public officials even though these books are public records. Harassment of persons exercising their rights as citizens to clean up the rolls has also been shown—for example, the threat by a deputy sheriff against Mrs. Lerly Murphy that her husband would be prosecuted for theft admittedly without grounds. Finally, we have sent statements by several Republican registrars who were purposely not trained by the County Court Clerk as required by law; you have a copy of the registrar's book for Precinct 28 which shows that the Clerk's Office tried to ignore the attempts of registrars attempting to purge the rolls. There is thus little doubt based on the evidence which our group as private citi-

224

zens, not investigative experts, has compiled to show that the registration rolls are improperly maintained by the legally responsible officials for the purpose of aiding in the effort to defraud the voters.

(3) *Fraud perpetrated by polling officials*: Many instances where polling officials (who are *experts* in defrauding voters) have clearly violated the law have been reported to your office. Secretary of State Robert Bailey's report confirmed our charges that several precincts presented serious discrepancies between the number of votes recorded on the machine and the corresponding number of poll slips; in fact, in one precinct (#73) an attempt was made by unauthorized persons to hand in all the books and poll slips secretly late; and in Precinct #59, the Republican poll slips have never turned up! The F.E.C. also sent you numerous affidavits concerning election officers who conversed, exchanged information, and left their stations with candidates and law enforcement officers for the purpose of manipulating the outcome of the election. You have much evidence (for example, in the statements of two polling officials from Precinct #46) that their co-workers used the excuse of "helping" voters with the machines to see how they voted and thereby confirm that the "bought voter" was really faithful.

(4) *Fraudulent absentee voting*: Once again local law enforcement and other State officials participated in acts of inducement to, and coercion against voters in order to have the election outcome under their control. Note the affidavit of Marion Davis that he was listed as voting absentee in person in the primary, but that he, in fact, voted absentee by mail, and the statements by Mrs. Betty Brinager and Mr. Okey Ray Spence that they witnessed numerous incidents of absentee vote fraud. Mr. Johnny Keesee, the Circuit Court Clerk, is quoted publicly as confirming their observations, as is Mr. John D. Rockefeller IV, who also observed the massive hauling and buying of absentee votes.

All of these incidents and the evidence submitted to you relate to past history. Now, we are again facing an urgent and pressing situation concerning the November 5 general election. Local and State officials have, since last spring's primary, been *totally unresponsive* to our efforts to prosecute violators of the election law. Efforts to steal this upcoming general election are already well underway. Here's the record:

(1) We have made efforts to secure the impaneling of a special grand jury from local and State officials. In response to our requests to the Governor and Attorney General of this State to use their legal authority and influence to help secure this investigation, we have not even received the formality of an acknowledgment of receipt of our letter. The prosecuting attorney of this county has taken no action on the evidence as forwarded to him for prosecutions by Secretary of State Robert Bailey.

(2) Several local officials, including a House of Delegates member, a candidate for Circuit Court Clerk, a Democratic District Committeeman, a Constable, and two State Road Commission employees have been charged with buying absentee votes. Affidavits on which these charges are based reveal that these officials have exerted pressure on, and/or offered inducement to, voters in order to sway their votes.

Based on the fact that no action has been taken to punish parties responsible for the past abuses which we have documented conclusively, and on the incontestable evidence that attempts are again being made to deprive the citizens of Mingo County of their voting rights, we urgently request that your office appoint federal observers to aid us in preventing abuses of the election process and, if necessary, in identifying and prosecuting those responsible for election fraud. We feel that your mandate is clear, and that the evidence justifying your use of this mandate is overwhelming. We, therefore, request that the Department of Justice act to insure justice to the voters of Mingo County, West Virginia.

16

The Monday following Smith's announce-
ment, I met with representatives from all of Mingo's community action groups. Everyone was disheartened and felt
that there was little that could be done to save the EOC. I
suggested that there was one last hope—to make it a state-
wide issue and get the two gubernatorial candidates
involved.

Chester Brown reacted, "I don't see how we could get
them involved. You take that Jim Sprouse; why, he's been
here in Mingo six times during the campaign, and he ain't
said 'dog' to the poor people. Every time he comes in, he
gets with Noah Floyd. You just can't trust a man like that."

"Yeah, I hear he even stays at Noah's house when he
comes to Mingo," chuckled James Washington.

Gladoula White said, "Well, you can't trust Moore
either. He's a Republican, and you know how they feel
about the poverty program. They've tried to defeat the bill
just about every time it comes up in Congress."

I interrupted, "I don't think we should concern ourselves with how they feel about the poverty program or
whether we can trust Sprouse. I think we must somehow

get them to make public statements supporting the EOC over the County Court. I personally believe we can convince Moore to support us, since he has nothing to lose and could only gain by it. Sprouse will be more difficult, since he has courted Noah so closely."

"You've got a good point there, Huey," William Mounts said, as he looked around for a reaction from the others.

"Yeah, it's a good point," agreed Herb Meade, "but I don't see how we could pull it off. Do you think for one moment that Sprouse would go against Noah and take a chance on losing the county?"

"You people know by now that the one thing a politician understands is people power," I replied, "and, if you can exert enough pressure on a politician, to the point where he feels it is going to hurt him, he will bend."

"I agree with you, but just how do you propose we will put enough pressure on them to make them bend?" James Washington said.

"Let me see if I can get a commitment from Moore, denouncing Smith's announcement, as soon as possible. This will put Sprouse on the defensive. Next, we could organize a mass protest on the steps of the State Capitol, denouncing Smith and the Democrats for casting the poor aside in favor of the Noah Floyd machine."

Washington said, "Well, I don't think we've got a thing to lose, and I am certainly game to try it. This governor's race is a seesaw battle according to everything I hear. It might just work."

Others agreed that we should proceed as quickly as possible with the plan. However, there was considerable skepticism about its potential success.

I suggested that we should be considering something

very dramatic for the demonstration in Charleston if the plan worked, such as a funeral cortege proclaiming the death of the poverty program. There was an enthusiastic response from William Mounts: "Hey, that's a good idea! Since Smith killed it, we could take it to the Capitol to bury it and have the funeral procession all the way from Williamson to Charleston, and invite others from all over the state to join us."

"We could have a hearse, with coffin and flowers, to lead the procession," chimed in Cletis Blackburn. "That would put the heat on them, and it's wild enough to get all sorts of publicity."

During the next few minutes, all sorts of suggestions were made regarding the procession. I sensed a new breath of life for the agency. It was agreed to maintain silence about our plan until we were successful in getting a statement from Moore.

The next morning, I came to the office early and drafted a statement from Moore to the OEO in Washington. At 10:00 A.M., I called his campaign headquarters in Charleston and spoke with Bill Loy, his administrative assistant. Loy, whom I had met previously in Williamson, was the only one in the Moore camp I knew. The receptionist told me that he was talking on another phone and that he would call me back. I explained that it was extremely important that I talk with him and asked if I could hold the line.

Shortly, Bill came to the phone. "What can I do for you?"

"I have a proposition I would like to throw at you," I replied.

"You know me; I am all ears," Bill said.

"You're aware, I'm sure, of the announcement Governor Smith made in Mingo Saturday night concerning the take-over of our poverty agency by the County Court."

"Yeah, I saw something in the paper about it."

"Well, I think Moore can make some mileage on it. If I read you a telegram I've drafted to OEO from Moore, you'll get the point."

There was no comment from Loy, perhaps because I did not give him time to comment. I began at once to read him the statement:

> Governor Hulett Smith designated the Mingo County Court as the community action agency for Mingo County. This decision was announced at a political rally sponsored by the Democratic Executive Committee of Mingo County. I personally must view the decision as being politically motivated.
>
> According to studies made by the Ford Foundation and an evaluation by the Office of Economic Opportunity, the Mingo County E.O.C. has an outstanding record in meeting the objectives of the Economic Opportunity Act of 1964. The innovative programs that have been developed by the staff and poor people, such as the full-year Head Start, home improvement, and other programs, clearly demonstrate that this agency has the ability to operate the poverty program.
>
> This agency has also stimulated a drive to eliminate election fraud within the democratic process, and is to be commended for its success and effort. The Mingo County Fair Elections Committee has won the praise and support of all West Virginians who advocate clean and honest elections.
>
> It is my opinion that designation of poverty agencies should be made solely upon the merits of the agency, whether it be a public agency such as a county court, or a non-profit agency such as the E.O.C., and the governor of the state should evaluate all factors before a decision is made, whether in Mingo County or in any other county within the state.

Therefore, I urge you to withhold any decision on Mingo County pending the outcome of the election, and I shall urge my Democratic opponent, James Sprouse, to take the same position.

When I finished, I said, "That's it. What do you think?"

"By God, I believe you have something there. I tell you what; put that in the mail to me immediately, and I'll show it to Arch as soon as I can." Then he interrupted his own line of thought: "No, better than that, why don't you bring it up to Charleston tonight and give it to him personally. He is speaking in Clarksburg and will be back here by 10:00 P.M."

"That's fine with me. I'll be there sharply at 10:00. Where do I come to?"

"Oh yes, he is staying at the Daniel Boone Hotel. Just ask the desk for the room number."

"O.K." I replied. "See you tonight."

That night, I waited in the lobby of the hotel until 1:00 A.M. Moore had been delayed in Clarksburg and had not returned until 12:30. As I rode the elevator to the eighth floor, I took several deep breaths to ease the tension. After straightening my tie, I knocked on the door.

Bill opened the door and invited me in. Across the room, Moore was sitting on a sofa, talking with another aide, Norman Yost. He immediately rose and walked across the room to greet me. There were heavy bags under his eyes; the final days of the campaign were beginning to show.

"Sorry to have kept you waiting so long," he said.

I replied, "No problem. I understand."

He then introduced me to Yost and yelled for his wife, who was in the bedroom: "Honey, would you come here a moment? I would like for you to meet someone."

Mrs. Moore came dressed in a housecoat. Like her husband, she extended her hand and said, "I am most delighted to meet you." After chatting a moment, she asked to be excused, and she returned to the bedroom, leaving the four of us alone.

Moore waited for me to bring up the subject. "I assume Bill has told you what I have proposed," I began.

"Yes, we talked briefly. Do you have the statement with you?"

"Yes," I replied, as I handed it to him from the inside of my coat pocket.

He read it carefully and, smiling broadly, said, "I'll send it tomorrow. In fact, I don't see anything that needs to be changed."

"How shall we handle the press release?" I asked. "Do you want me to do it, or would you prefer one of your men to do it?"

"Why don't you take care of it?" he replied. "You seem to have better access to the press than we do." He smiled again.

"That's fine with me. And now I'll leave and let you get some rest. I appreciate the position you have taken, and I am sure the poor people of Mingo will appreciate it."

He walked with me to the door, where we shook hands again. Bill yelled across the room, "See you later, Perry."

It was 1:30 when I began my drive back to Williamson. I had thought of staying in Charleston, but it was important to get back to the office in order to prepare the press release. The following day, Moore's statement was carried across the state. The first phase of our plan was complete.

With time running out, we immediately began the second phase—an endorsement from James Sprouse.

Cletis Blackburn arranged to borrow a hearse and a casket from a funeral director in Kentucky. Within forty-eight hours, the community action groups enlisted more than 500 of the county's poor and 150 cars to participate in the hundred-mile funeral cortege we had planned. And, on the heels of the Moore announcement, I released the story to the *Charleston Gazette*, explaining the purpose of the funeral procession as a denunciation of Governor Smith's decision. During the late afternoon, I began to receive numerous telephone calls from all over the state, supporting the procession and asking whether others could participate. The funeral services were scheduled for 2:00 P.M., November 1—four days before the general election.

On October 30, I received a call from Vito Stagliano, our new field representative, who explained that the OEO was being flooded with telephone calls from the statehouse, demanding that the funeral procession be called off. Vito said, "In fact, Perry, it is only fair for me to tell you that, if you go through with it, the OEO will withdraw your funds."

"What the hell have we got to lose?" I asked. "They will give them to Noah Floyd February first, anyway. Whose side are you on?"

"I am on your side, but you must understand it is not me that is making the demand. I am only relating to you what I've been told."

"Well, you relate back that the funeral procession is on and, as far as I am concerned, the OEO can go to hell!" I shouted into the telephone.

Vito said, "I am meeting with the Sprouse and Smith people tomorrow. I will call you from Charleston."

I replied, "You tell Sprouse that, if he will publicly rescind Smith's decision and recognize the EOC if he is elected governor, we will call off the funeral. Remind him of Smith's statement where he said, 'Everything is out of OEO's hands now.' "

I sensed that Vito was upset with my tone of voice and uncompromising attitude, but I had no choice. I had expected Smith to apply pressure on the OEO and interpreted it as meaning that the plan was working and the Sprouse camp was now beginning to feel the pressure. Otherwise, they would have ignored the funeral procession.

The following day, I received a call from Jim McIntire, Sprouse's campaign manager. He explained that he was aware of our concern and that he would discuss the matter with Sprouse and tell me the decision as soon as possible. I gave him all the telephone numbers where he could reach me at different times.

The Sprouse camp did not get in touch with us until 9:00 P.M., and then only through a call from Vito, who said that Sprouse had not arrived but Paul Crabtree, Jim McIntire, Miles Stanley, and several others were meeting now, and they were primarily waiting for Sprouse's return. He added, "Paul Crabtree is madder than hell. He came into the meeting about thirty minutes ago and said, 'The Governor is not going to give in to Perry's eleventh-hour blackmail.' "

"That's beautiful."

"Perry, you sure have them worried. Miles Stanley is arguing for a statement to recognize the EOC, but he is meeting opposition from Crabtree and some of Sprouse's aides," Vito continued.

I was glad to hear that Stanley was supporting us. He was the president of the West Virginia AFL-CIO, and he was strongly endorsing Sprouse, who had been legal counsel for the unions.

Vito said that he would call me as soon as anything developed and that he wanted me to remain at the office. By now, Crabtree had issued a statement to the press claiming that the demonstration was based on a misunderstanding: "The governor is merely clarifying that the County Court indicated a desire to designate itself and that they have the statutory power to do so under the legislation passed by the legislature." He continued, "The governor does not have the power of designation under the federal Green Amendment, and, at a news conference six months ago, he said he felt the private, nonprofit operation of these agencies would be more desirable."

Crabtree's statement only added fuel to our fire. Through Vito, I had earlier received a copy of Smith's letter to Astor Kirk, the OEO regional director, and there was no doubt about the contents of the letter and its meaning. Smith wrote to Kirk:

> In September, Mr. Edward S. Cogen, then Acting Regional Director, advised me of the counties which had met deadlines for designating themselves as the community action agencies, and our records show these to be Webster, Raleigh, and Mingo Counties.
>
> In the previous applications for designation by these County Courts, there was some question raised as to whether or not, under the State Economic Opportunity Act and the statutes governing County Courts, the County would have the authority and power to become an effective community action agency.
>
> At our special session of the West Virginia Legislature, under an act amending Chapter 7, Article 13 of the West Virginia Code, a new section was added which authorized and empowered the County Court to become a community action program, organization or agency pursuant to Title II of the Federal Economic Opportunity Act of 1964.

With this action of the Legislature, there is no doubt in my mind that the County Courts now have full power in becoming a community action agency; and I would, therefore, recognize the actions of the Mingo, Raleigh and Webster County Courts' designation of themselves as the community action agency to replace the existing one in each County under the terms of the Community Action Amendments, known as the Green Amendment.

While I was concerned with the negotiations in Charleston, other staff members were busy coordinating the funeral procession. It was scheduled to depart from Cinderella at 9:00 the next morning.

At 11:00 P.M., I received another call from Vito. He informed me that there was no break in the meeting. They were still deadlocked. Sprouse had just arrived, and he was now involved in the discussion. Vito gave me a telephone number where he could be reached.

At 1:00 A.M., I called Vito and told him I was going to bed and could not be reached until the next morning. "You tell them, unless I get a call before 9:00 A.M., the funeral cannot be stopped." Those were my final words before I left the office.

At 8:30 A.M., I came back to the office, to find about 200 cars with about 800 people—many more than we had anticipated—lined up along Cinderella hollow. Cletis had parked the hearse at the mouth of the hollow. Several people asked if I had heard anything from Sprouse, and I said that I hadn't heard anything positive.

I looked at my watch. It was now 8:50. It certainly appeared that the Sprouse camp was unable to reach a decision. I had almost given up hope of a phone call when, at 8:55, Jim McIntire called.

Wearily, he said, "Perry, we have reached the decision to

recognize the existing EOC as the official poverty agency if Jim is elected."

He was in no mood for a lengthy discussion. I thanked him for his decision and immediately ran outside to tell the people.

Excitement ran from one end of the hollow to the other. "We've won! We've won!" people were yelling. Others chanted, "Death to the County Court!"

Thirty minutes later, the assembled mourners decided to take the procession through the county to celebrate the victory. The sign reading "Death of the Poverty Program" was taken from the hearse, and a hastily lettered sign reading "Death of the County Court" put in its place.

On February 12, 1969, the EOC received the following from the OEO:

The 1967 Amendments to the Economic Opportunity Act of 1964 provided local political jurisdictions with the opportunity to determine the agency which would serve that jurisdiction as the community action agency charged with the overall responsibility of planning, coordinating and administering anti-poverty activities. Pursuant to those Amendments, the county officials of Mingo County were given the opportunity to designate a community action agency in accordance with the implementing regulations promulgated by O.E.O.

As you know, the West Virginia Economic Opportunity Act of 1965 requires that all community action agencies in the State be approved by the Governor.

The Economic Opportunity Commission has won [the] Governor's approval.

Therefore, pursuant to Section 210(d) of the Economic Opportunity Act, I have designated the Economic Opportunity Commission as the anti-poverty agency for Mingo County.

17

Although the Mingo County EOC had been successful in opposing the take-over of the antipoverty agency by the County Court, 1969 saw the growth of much apprehension among the poor of the county. Practically everyone who had been involved in the war on poverty believed that the new Nixon Administration would not continue with the OEO—or that, at least, it would restructure the program in such a way that it would become ineffective. There seemed good reason to fear for the survival of the Mingo County EOC, which had become the rural model for liberals in the Democratic Administration, and now, with the Nixon Administration, would probably be regarded as the prime example of "how not to do it."

The new instructions we were receiving from the OEO were mostly concerned with rules of management that de-emphasized involvement of poor people in decision-making; we were told that we were to involve all segments of the county in policy decisions and in the administration of community action programs. In addition, criticism soon began to be leveled against those poverty agencies that had been successful in organizing the poor, based on claims that they had succeeded only in splitting communities and had disrupted activities of locally established institutions that had served well in the past. Demonstrations and protests against elected officials would now result in a withdrawal of federal funds, we were told. In Mingo County, this could only mean an end to the Fair Elections Committee and the Committee for Education. It was impossible for either of them to operate without some financial assistance from the EOC.

I was determined to work for one more year. Before the exodus of most of our friends from OEO, the Mingo County EOC had received a two-year research and demonstration grant of $150,000. It was designed to create nonprofit businesses that would employ welfare recipients. My plan was to work entirely with this program.

There was some comfort in the fact that, at least for the time being, the local politicians were not publicly attacking the EOC. Their failure to take over the agency had hurt their prestige in the county, and Noah was preoccupied with his new position in the state Senate. He had been appointed chairman of the Senate committee on elections by an old friend of his, Senate President Lloyd Jackson. Jackson was from the same school of politicians as Noah, and Noah probably had made a request for the position.

Because the committee was charged with the responsibility of strengthening the state election laws to prevent fraud, Noah's appointment was considered a slap in the face for the Mingo County Fair Elections Committee, as well as a personal blow to Jay Rockefeller, who, as the newly elected secretary of state of West Virginia, had wasted no time in submitting to the Senate committee his recommendations for election law changes. His proposals came after a series of public hearings throughout the state concerning electoral fraud and after consultation with the Fair Elections Committee.

The first public hearing had been held in Mingo County and was viewed by many as an effort to embarrass Noah, but, because the secretary of state did not have either the power to subpoena witnesses or the legal power to follow up in court, the hearings were scarcely more important than the many other meetings that had been conducted by the Fair Elections Committee. They did, however, attract a considerable amount of newspaper publicity, which kept the issue of fraud before the public.

It was satisfying to see Jay pick up the fight for election reform, whatever the results. But, in spite of all his efforts, the state Senate election committee did not respond to his suggestions or attempt to reform the law. Floyd contended that the existing law was adequate, and he unleashed in the press a bitter attack against Rockefeller.

The hearings were soon overshadowed by the convening of a federal grand jury in Huntington, West Virginia, which Jay Rockefeller had been instrumental in getting the Justice Department to call. Before Ramsey Clark vacated his position as U.S. attorney general, Jay went to Washington and encouraged Clark to intensify the Department's efforts to substantiate the electoral fraud that had been uncovered by the Mingo County Fair Elections Committee. In late March, after the 1968 general election, practically all of the elected officials in the county except Noah were subpoenaed to testify.

The special grand jury was in session for two days. After its investigation, word spread that Ernest Ward, a former deputy sheriff, had "spilled the beans on Noah." After the election, Governor Arch Moore, a Republican, had diverted county jobs to the local Republican organization, and Noah had a difficult time finding enough jobs for all of his friends. Even the creation of several new janitorial jobs in the courthouse, along with an assortment of other new positions paid for by county funds, was not enough to take care of displaced state workers. Ward was angry with Noah because he had not been able to get him the county job he wanted. The loss of patronage had tended to splinter the local Democratic party generally. Tom Chafin had formed an alliance with former Sheriff Steve Adkins, who had just vacated his office, and their goal was to wrest control of the Democratic Party from Noah. They were eagerly making friends with Noah's enemies. As a result, Tom had hired Ward as a deputy clerk in his office.

It was this split in the Democratic Party that prompted Ward to relate to me what had happened at the grand jury investigation. He did so one day when I was transacting personal business at the courthouse in Williamson. Chafin and Ward were unusually friendly to me that day. Both assured me that they were now on my side and were going to work for fair elections.

After saying hello, Ward nudged my shoulder and said, "I sure laid it on that son of a bitch Noah down at Huntington."

"Yeah, what happened?" I asked, pumping for information.

"Well, to tell you the truth, I didn't have much choice."

Tom was standing beside Ward, grinning from ear to ear. I could not help thinking back to the time, a few months earlier, when we had been bitter enemies as a result of the activities of the Fair Elections Committee. But such is the nature of Appalachian politics that here I was standing beside him, listening to his assistant tell me how he had got his revenge on Noah.

Ward continued, "You see, it was like this. When that fellow, Brown, from the Department of Justice put me on the stand, I felt I had better tell the truth 'cause I didn't want to spend time for perjury. God, he was rough! I guess I was going along fairly well until he pulled out this big picture of me and T. I. Varney. I knew then there was nothing left for me to do but tell the truth. Besides, the way that Goddamn son of a bitch Noah had lied to me made me want to put his ass behind bars, anyway."

Although two or three other people, including a deputy sheriff, walked over to where we were standing, Ward was not silenced and continued to relate his story. Tom, I am sure, had heard it several times already, but he appeared to be as enthusiastic as the others. Ward became very dramatic as he began to act out the courtroom scene, first pretending to be Brown from the Justice Department and then giving his own answers to Brown's questions.

"Brown held that picture right up in front of me and said, 'Do you know these two men?' "

" 'Yes, sir,' I said, 'That's me and T. I. Varney.' "

" 'Where were you when this picture was taken?' "

" 'We were coming out of Noah Floyd's house.' "

" 'When?' "

" 'It was the Sunday before the general election.' "

" 'Would you tell me what you were carrying?' "

" 'It's a brown paper sack.' "

" 'Was there anything in it?' "

" 'Yes.' "

" 'What?' "

" 'Money.' "

" 'How much?' "

" 'To tell you the truth, Mr. Brown, I don't remember if there was fourteen hundred dollars or fifteen hundred dollars.' "

" 'Where did you get it?' "

" 'From Noah Floyd.' "

" 'What did you use it for?' "

" 'To buy votes in Magnolia District.' "

Ward chuckled as he remembered the courtroom scene. Shaking his head from side to side, he said, "I'll tell you, Perry, T. I. is scared to death. I wouldn't do anything to hurt T. I. Why, we were raised up together. Anyway, I've been having some fun out of him. He keeps telling me nothing will ever happen. To tell you the truth, I think we are all in trouble. I know they will send me up. I've been there before. The only thing I want them to do is put Noah straight across from me so I can stand and look at him."

Tom laughed and slapped his hands together. "Yes sir, Cuz, things are going to be a little different now, and I would like to work with you."

Tom called everyone he talked with "Cuz." In fact, he claimed to be a cousin to everyone, and, as a result, he was probably the most popular politician in the county.

"We've got to beat Noah the next time," he continued. "You know he runs again in 1970."

I only grinned. However, I am sure he interpreted that to mean that I would help him.

Ernest, laying his hand on my shoulder, said, "They got hold of Arnold Starr's little black book where he had listed all the money he had taken in from the flower fund." (The "flower fund," as it was called by local politicians, contained the forced contributions of all the state and county employees. The average contribution was $10 a month, but some of the high-salaried employees were required to pay as much as $20 a month. If an employee failed to contribute, he was dismissed.) "Well, that's no problem. The problem comes when he has to tell what he did with it. And everybody knows he gave it to Noah to distribute."

I left the courthouse somewhat startled and confused by what I had heard. It was apparent that Noah's machine was falling apart, and that fact alone made me happy.

As time passed, the break in the local political machine became more apparent. Jay Rockefeller was extremely disturbed by Floyd's efforts to thwart election reform at the state level and, out of expediency, turned to the dissident group of Mingo Democrats headed by Tom Chafin to seek a candidate to oppose Noah in the upcoming primary.

Finding a candidate was no easy task. Usually, the private meetings included arguments among potential candidates, each claiming he had the most voter- strength. But after two or three meetings, the field was narrowed to two potential candidates—former sheriff Howard Chambers and former school board member Lafe Ward. Jay was in a quandary as to how to solve the problem and still maintain unity within the dissident group. On two occasions he sought my advice, and, in fact, he invited me to attend the meeting at which the final decision would be made. Although I was certainly not impressed by either candidate, I suggested that Ward would probably run the best race against Floyd.

After much persuasion from Jay, Chambers decided to back down and run for the House of Delegates, thus setting the stage for a showdown with Floyd. As the election approached, Jay spent most of his time campaigning for Ward in McDowell County because it was included with Mingo in the senatorial district. Ward was not expected to win Mingo, and the strategy was to gain a fairly substantial majority of votes in McDowell to offset his Mingo loss.

Floyd's strategy was to attack Rockefeller personally, labeling him as "a rich outsider whose only interest is to become governor of West Virginia." West Virginia, he said, "is only a stepping stone to the White House." Floyd said very little regarding his opponent, Lafe Ward, during the entire campaign.

It was a heated election—and probably as crooked as any ever held in Mingo—and Floyd lost by a very small margin. However, he maintained control over the Democratic Executive Committee, and, in Mingo County, this meant he was still the political boss.

After the election, I began to devote most of my time to the newly funded economic development program and laid the groundwork for the establishment of a moccasin factory that would employ thirty-five welfare recipients. It was an extremely time-consuming process, but the factory was established within three months, and a training program for welfare mothers to make moccasins was implemented. The factory was incorporated as a nonstock corporation, with all of the profits going back into the parent Economic Development Corporation.

Using the same corporate structure, two other businesses were established—a gourmet restaurant that employed twelve former welfare recipients in Williamson, and a nonprofit grocery store in Gilbert. Both aroused resentment from the established businessmen because the enterprises were financed with federal funds. The biggest complaint against the restaurant was directed at the $1.60-an-hour wage scale for its employees. Other restaurants in town paid only $25 per week for six 10-hour days. An emergency food supplement program operated by the EOC added to the controversy. The EOC was assisting welfare recipients with the purchase of their food stamps, and many of these people were buying their groceries at the poverty store. Charges were made that food stamp recipients were being forced to spend their food stamps at the store as a prerequisite for receiving the supplemental grant from the emergency food program. These charges were absurd. However, it was difficult to convince the businessmen that poor people supported the store simply because prices were low and they also knew that profits would eventually be spent on other projects that would benefit them.

All during this period, the FBI continued to investigate electoral fraud in the county, and several businessmen and politicians took advantage of the opportunity to include the Mingo County EOC in the investigation. Numerous letters had been written to Senator Byrd complaining that the restaurant and grocery store were running "legitimate" businesses bankrupt. Two grocery store owners in Gilbert had hired two local attorneys to investigate the Gilbert grocery store and the emergency food program. Their investigation resulted in a letter to President Richard Nixon complaining about the use of federal funds to establish businesses for low income people, which they described as being discriminatory against the "legitimate" businesses that were paying taxes to support the poverty programs. Local courthouse politicians had also complained to the FBI that they were being victimized by the poverty agency and that federal funds were being used only to embarrass the local Democratic Party. They demanded an investigation of the EOC. Their strategy evidently was to make the EOC, as accuser, look as guilty as the accused. I was the target of their wrath.

I should have realized at the time that an investigation by the FBI was imminent. The power of local politicians did not stop at the county lines, and I had always believed Senator Robert Byrd to be the Washington extension of county political bosses throughout southern West Virginia. I remember that, when I learned what was pending, or rumored to be pending, I thought, "How simple it would be for Byrd to pick up the phone and tell J. Edgar Hoover that he wanted the EOC investigated, especially if he had scores of letters charging the misuse of federal funds, such as the one the lawyers sent to President Nixon."

However, I continued to ignore the possibility until one morning I found myself surrounded by no fewer than half a dozen federal marshals and FBI agents. They were armed with subpoenas from the U.S. Court of Southern West Virginia, demanding all the records of the EOC and the poverty grocery store. The employees of the EOC were immediately placed under surveillance, and agents situated themselves at all entrances, as if we were all hardened criminals ready to attempt escape.

Within thirty minutes, I received a call from R. F. Copley, the manager of the Gilbert grocery store. R. F. had been fired as a bus driver by the Board of Education because of his activist role in organizing the union. On account of his previous experience as a grocery store manager during the 1940's, we had hired him for the Gilbert store. As I picked up the phone, one of the agents moved as close as possible, making an effort to overhear the conversation.

R. F. was excited. "What the hell is going on, Perry? There's a man standing here with a badge, wanting our records. What should I do?"

I replied, "Let him have them."

As I talked, the agent moved closer, and I purposely held the phone closer to my head in an effort to shut off the conversation.

R. F. said, "It's hard for me to talk with you. This feller is awful nosey. He's got his head stuck right up here in this phone trying to hear what we are talking about."

"Don't feel lonesome," I said, "I've got the same problem on this end."

He asked, "What do you figure has caused this?"

"I don't know. I can guess it is either the politicians or the local merchants."

He replied, "Well, I'll talk to you later, when we have some privacy. In the meantime, I'll send this feller to see Cline, our bookkeeper, since he has all our records."

"Fine," I replied.

It was almost noon before the agents finished loading the records into a rental truck. Everything was taken, including pamphlets, correspondence, accounting records, and all loose papers lying around. There was very little I could say to encourage the staff. Everyone just stood around in total disbelief. One of the agents frowned at me when I told a staff member that I guessed this was the kind of treatment you had to expect when you worked to help the poor.

At that point, I received a call from Wilford Cline, who was the store accountant and a full-time high school teacher at Gilbert. He was more concerned with what one of the marshals had said to him than he was with the confiscation of the records. "Huey, I've never seen anything like it. This man took me out of class and has treated me as if I were a criminal. What really made me mad though was his reference to how dirty the school building was. As we were walking down the hall, he said, 'This is as dirty as a "nigger" school.'"

"I certainly hope he is not typical of federal agents," I said.

"Can you imagine the man making a statement like that?"

"It is difficult. Well, don't worry about it now. Give them the records. Do they want you to go to Charleston?"

"Yes," he answered. "They want me to identify the records before a federal grand jury."

"Okay, I'll see you there, since I have to do the same thing for the EOC records."

(The marshal later wrote to the West Virginia Superintendent of Schools, complaining about the unsanitary conditions of the Gilbert school. A copy of the letter was sent to the high school principal, who became extremely angry about the charge.)

As I drove to Charleston that afternoon, many thoughts ran through my mind. The entire experience was unbelievable. I had been aware that FBI agents had questioned several community people in Dingess concerning the possible misuse of the emergency food program during the general election, but I had not considered it a serious matter. Nevertheless, I had questioned Oscar Dingess, the EOC employee in charge of the program in Dingess, along with Leo Dent, a member of the community group who was on the local community committee that determined who was eligible to receive assistance. Both had assured me that there had been no wrongdoings and that the whole thing was just a rumor started by some of Noah's friends in the community to get back at the Fair Elections Committee. Several people from the Dingess community had appeared before the grand jury in Huntington, but I could not conceive of any evidence submitted that would implicate the EOC in electoral fraud.

I was also aware that FBI agents had been told that I had gone to Dingess on election day and had personally made out emergency food checks to the people in the area in exchange for their votes. The EOC accountant had been thoroughly questioned concerning the procedure in writing checks for the emergency food program. She had explained that she had written all the checks after the community group had submitted a list of eligible names. Although it had been disgusting to hear described the questioning procedure used by the FBI, I had shrugged off the entire matter and believed the agents would be satisfied once they determined that it was all rumor.

My greatest concern was the effect that the seizure of the records by the FBI would have on the poverty agency and its programs. All of the women who worked in the accounting office spent the next two days, along with me, in Charleston identifying the records. I was questioned by the grand jury as to whether I owned any part of the grocery store. I explained that it was impossible for anyone to own any part of the store, because it was incorporated as a non-stock corporation. It belonged to the poor people. I further told the grand jury that they should investigate the other grocery stores in the area if they were going to investigate real violations. I told the jury that, before there had been a poverty store, people had been paying 10 per cent more for several items and that many of the store owners had profiteered in the government food stamp program by giving recipients as little as $10 for a twenty-dollar book of stamps. The grand jury did not respond to that statement, and I was dismissed after about thirty minutes of questioning. The corrupt-election charges were not mentioned.

When it appeared that our records were going to be impounded indefinitely, the agency hired a Charleston attorney to prepare a petition against the U.S. attorney to force the court to return the records. For more than sixty days, we had been attempting to operate a two million–dollar federal program without records. On the very day the petition was filed, the records were released.

FBI agents continued to visit the county on a regular basis, asking poor people what they thought of me as an individual and whether they believed that I would buy votes with the emergency food monies. On several occasions, community action leaders were asked if they thought communists had infiltrated the EOC. All my personal records, such as bank accounts and court records, were examined. It was difficult to maintain my composure, and I was positive that, if the harassment continued, many of the county residents would begin to lose confidence in me and in the poverty agency. Regardless of how honest a poverty agency was, it was easy to create suspicion when there were implications being made by the FBI about possible misuse of poverty money.

Three months after the release of the records, another federal grand jury was convened, and all the project directors of the EOC were subpoenaed to testify. The fact that I had not been subpoenaed indicated that a presentment against me would have been made if any evidence could have been gathered to substantiate the rumors. The session lasted only one day, but it became quite clear, because of the questions asked, that everything was directed toward me. I was the recognized leader of the poor, and it was probably concluded that there would be no more problems in the county if I could somehow be eliminated. Practically all the witnesses who appeared believed that I was the only person being sought in the agency.

I was told that the local politicians in the county, and several outside the county, were thoroughly enjoying the pressures being applied by the FBI. However, their spirits were soon dampened.

On August 5, 1970, a federal grand jury, meeting secretly in Bluefield, West Virginia, finally returned indictments against Noah Floyd, T. I. Varney, Harry Artis, and Arnold Starr. The indictments, which were announced by Attorney General John Mitchell, charged that the four politicians had conspired to influence the outcome of the November general election in 1968. It further charged that the four had misused $50,000 in the process of influencing the election.

In Mingo County, crooked elections had been a way of life. Down through the years, thousands of county residents had been involved. There was hardly a household up the creeks and hollows that did not know the meaning of electoral fraud. And hundreds of people now feared that they would be next to be indicted. Electoral fraud was not confined to the poor. It reached much farther, into the county's professional class. Schoolteachers and attorneys and others had also been instrumental in perpetuating the fraudulent electoral system in Mingo County.

Many people expected high-ranking politicians in Washington, particularly Congressman Jim Kee and Senator Robert Byrd, to intervene and somehow get the indictments quashed. Their reasoning was simple: Noah had always supported these men during the elections, and they could always count on receiving 80 per cent of the total vote of the county. When a vote was bought, it was bought for them also. However, there was total silence. No high-ranking politician uttered a word publicly in defense of Noah.

It was almost a year later when the four politicians were brought to trial. By then, I had left the EOC and gone to work on an OEO-supported low-cost housing program in Charleston. But, of course, I followed the trial with intense interest.

Zane Grey Staker represented the defense. As expected, the U.S. Government relied primarily on the testimony of Ernest Ward, who had been named as a coconspirator but not as a codefendant. During the trial's second day, Ward was questioned once again by U.S. Attorney Edgar Brown, and he gave the same testimony he had given to the grand jury. He also related a conversation he had had with defendant Arnold Starr after the indictment was handed down. Ward said Starr expressed concern about the "predicament" Floyd had gotten him into. He explained that Starr was afraid that adverse publicity could cause him to lose his preaching license. Ward then told the jury that he had bought between 100 and 150 votes.

Cross-examined by Staker, Ward admitted that a political rift had developed between Floyd and himself. He also admitted making the statement "Even if I have to go to the penitentiary myself, I'll get Noah Floyd." During the entire cross-examination, Staker continued to elaborate on the political rift that had developed.

Two ex–deputy sheriffs also gave incriminating evidence against the defendants. Jimmy Hatfield, a burly thirty-two-year-old coal miner, told the jury he had been asked by Floyd to buy votes in his precinct. He said he had bought 30 to 35 votes and paid as much as $5 for them in some cases. He also claimed he had been coached by Floyd before the 1968 election in the art of buying votes.

Under cross-examination, Hatfield denied an allegation by the defense attorney, Zane Grey Staker, that he harbored a grudge against Floyd for his failure to gain the party's backing as a nominee for justice of the peace in 1968.

The other ex–deputy sheriff, Thomas Jefferson Copley, testified that he had worked as a Democratic precinct captain in the 1968 elections and had received on both occasions $550 in one-dollar bills from Noah Floyd to be used for buying votes. Copley told the court how he and another Democratic worker had prepared for the primary and general elections and described stuffing small envelopes with $3 in one-dollar bills and purchasing liquor and wine, all to be used in buying votes. His testimony also directly implicated Artis, who, he said, had supplied him with more money on election day when his original sum had been exhausted. At one point in his testimony, Copley claimed that 90 per cent of his precinct's votes had been bought. He also told of buying the votes of a preacher and his family the night before the election.

Under cross-examination by Staker, Copley admitted that he had been forced by Artis to resign his deputy's post but said he bore no ill feelings against Artis, whom he described as "like a father to me."

During the eight days of testimony, all the defendants proclaimed their innocence.

Floyd said he "deplored vote buying."

T. I. Varney, asked if he had participated in an exchange of money in connection with vote buying, answered, "Emphatically no!"

Artis also claimed he had never been involved in vote fraud.

Arnold Starr, the preacher, was never placed on the witness stand by the defense.

Other county officials, including two County Court commissioners, W. A. "Shorty" Myers and C. J. Hamilton, said they had not witnessed vote buying in 1968. Both men said they had attended meetings at Floyd's home before the election and had received money to be used for various election expenses. When Hamilton was asked if that money could have been used to buy votes, he said, "We get credit for a lot of things up there we don't do."

On the eighth day, the testimony was concluded, and the prosecution and defense presented their final arguments. United States Attorney Brown, from the Justice Department, said, "Freedom has been lost in Mingo County. There is a government of the organization, by the organization, and for the organization."

Brown contended that the government had produced evidence that vote buying had taken place. "These offices are bought and sold," he said. "The only thing people get when they go to the polls in Mingo County is money."

Zane Grey Staker, for the defense, did not say much. He simply characterized the key witnesses for the government as "thugs, thieves, and hoodlums" and told the jury that the case boiled down to a matter of witness credibility.

The jury deliberated nearly three hours before returning to the tensely silent court room. Then the foreman stood and announced the verdict for each defendant individually.

In all four cases, the verdict was "not guilty."

When all four verdicts had been read, there were, I am told, audible sighs and joyful tears in the court room. Leaving the court with their families and friends, Noah Floyd and the other defendants smiled and expressed their gratitude.

Harry Artis said, "I thank God we still have justice in this country."

About the Authors

Huey Perry, a native of Mingo County, West Virginia, was named Director of the Mingo County Economic Opportunity Commission project at the age of 29. He is an author, entrepreneur, teacher, student, volunteer, chairman, business owner, and farmer.

Jeff Biggers is the American Book Award-winning author of *The United States of Appalachia* and *Reckoning at Eagle Creek: The Secret Legacy of Coal in the Heartland*.

CPSIA information can be obtained
at www.ICGtesting.com
Printed in the USA
LVOW04s0117151116
512983LV00027B/481/P